MORE
MACABRE
MISCELLANY

Geoffrey Abbott is a Yeoman Warder (retd), HM Tower of London, and member of The Sovereign's Bodyguard of the Yeoman of the Guard Extraordinary.

MORE
MACABRE
MISCELLANY

An all new collection of 1,000 hideous and horrifying facts

Geoffrey Abbott

Dedicated to my newly discovered half-sister Helen.
What a delightful surprise!

First published in Great Britain in 2005 by
Virgin Books Ltd
Thames Wharf Studios
Rainville Road
London
W6 9HA

A catalogue record for this book is available from
the British Library.

ISBN 0 7535 1022 7

Typeset by Phoenix Photosetting, Chatham, Kent
Printed and bound in Great Britain by
Bookmarque Ltd

CONTENTS

INTRODUCTION

Herewith another batch of macabre facts for the discerning reader who likes to garner his or her information in small chunks ready to hand, rather than have to wade through pages and pages of magazines and books before coming across a really bizarre nugget. All the items are real and genuine; the human race, thank heavens, is a conglomeration, a hotchpotch of people who do weird things, such as practising for death by sleeping in their coffins, or wearing a diamond ring made out of their husband's ashes, or have even weirder things happen to them, like suddenly talking in a long-lost language or being rained on by fish.

All this little book seeks to do is hold up a mirror, for all to see the odd, the strange, the macabre events that have happened across the world, across the country – sometimes, perhaps, even in the house next door! Herein you will find fascinating anecdotes about royalty and hangmen, superstitions and ancient punishments, nauseating medical cures and crazy inventions; you will discover what a merkin is, and what you are afraid of if you have Taphephobia.

We suggest that you ration yourself; just peruse a page or two a day, shake your head slowly at the antics that other people get up to – and then take all the necessary precautions to avoid becoming eligible for inclusion in a third edition of this book!

BONES, BRAINS AND BODY-PARTS

A letter from a reader appeared in an 1829 issue of the magazine *Lion* describing how he wanted his body disposed of after death. Rather than waste anything, he stated that his bones should be carved into knife- and walking-stick handles, his skin tanned into leather with which to cover an armchair, and his flesh mixed with earth and used as a compost for a flower-bed.

Charlie Chaplin's body was stolen from the Swiss cemetery in which it had been buried in 1978. A ransom was demanded but not paid. The corpse was found weeks later buried in a field ten miles away. The grave robbers were given long prison sentences.

Prime Minister Spencer Perceval was killed in 1812 by John Bellingham, who was hanged and dissected. Afterwards his skull somehow went astray and was not found until 1962, in the anatomy storeroom of St Bartholomew's Hospital, London.

William Corder murdered Maria Marten in 1828. The whereabouts of her body, in the Red Barn, were revealed in a dream to her mother. Corder was hanged and dissected, pieces of his skin were sold as souvenirs and his skeleton was put on display in a glass case in a nearby hospital, its arm rising to point to a collection box whenever visitors approached.

Among the archives in the Carnavalet Museum in Paris is a 1793 copy of the French Constitution – bound in human skin.

During the reign of Charles I, the Jesuit Fr Barlow was hanged, quartered and boiled in tar. Parts of his body were retrieved by believers and in 1746 a wooden chest was found in an old mansion in Lancashire containing his skull, which, it was believed, had supernatural powers and would bring misfortune if treated with disrespect.

Far from ordering the sea to retreat, King Canute was simply demonstrating to his followers that not even a king could control the waves. In 1951 archaeologists involved in a dig in Shaftesbury discovered a glass bowl containing a heart believed to be his.

Workmen digging in Ozone Park, New York, in October 2004 uncovered human remains, which were identified as those of two Mafia bosses who had been 'eliminated' twenty years before.

In Auld Ireland, a youth wishing to make himself irresistible to a girl would steal a hair from her head, thread it on a needle and pass it through a dead man's arm or leg. After that, it is averred, the girl was his, begorrah!

After being defeated at the Battle of Stoke in 1487, Lord Lovell hid in an underground room in his home, Minster Lovell. For reasons unknown, the servant having the room's key left the area and, when the chamber was discovered two hundred years later, his Lordship's skeleton was found still seated in a chair.

The corpse of the English martyr Sir John Southworth, dismembered in 1654, was later sewn together and buried in Westminster Abbey.

In Scotland Yard's Black Museum are, among other gory artefacts, a brain preserved in formaldehyde, the severed arms of a murderer, a skeletal hand and a large number of death masks taken from hanged criminals.

Where injuries following an attack were concerned, the Anglo-Saxons had a scale of fines depending on which of 34 parts of the body had been affected, based on the 'usefulness' of that part. So, for example, an attacker severing a victim's 'middlemost' finger would be fined 12 shillings but for a 'shooting' finger (forefinger) 15 shillings. The fine for breaking someone's arms was the huge sum of 30 shillings.

Professor Buckland, an eminent osteologist, discovered that the relics of St Rosalia in Palermo, which had for ages reputedly cured disciples of diseases and warded off fearsome epidemics, were the bones of a goat. Nevertheless hundreds of believers continued to visit the site.

Settlers in the American Ozarks believed that powder made by grinding the bones of an old corpse, when sprinkled on the sores, was a certain cure for syphilis.

In the sixteenth century many Italian artists helped surgeons to dissect corpses so that they could draw or sculpt nude figures more accurately.

After defeating the Mahdi's army in the nineteenth century, Lord Kitchener of Khartoum desecrated his enemy's remains by using his skull as an inkwell.

Sir Thomas Blount was sentenced to be hanged, drawn and quartered for high treason in the fourteenth century. It was reported that on the scaffold 'the executioner knelt down and opened his belly and cut his bowels straight from below the stomach and tied them with a string, that the wind of the heart should not escape, and threw the bowels into the fire. His head was then cut off and he was quartered.'

After his death in 1637 the famous poet Ben Jonson was buried in an upright position in Westminster Abbey. One explanation is that he wished to be standing ready for the Resurrection.

A skull believed to be that of Tom Paine, the eighteenth-century religious and political radical, was bought at an auction in Australia in 1988.

The operators of a crematorium in a certain Lancashire town cremate corpses weighing over 250lb before 9.30 a.m., otherwise the furnaces overheat and block the jets with ash.

After the coronation of James II in 1685, workmen dismantling the scaffolding round the viewing stands accidentally dropped a beam of wood on the top of the shrine of Edward the Confessor, breaking a hole in it, through which could be seen the head of the royal corpse. A lawyer, Henry Keepe, later inserted his hand, rummaged among the bones and extracted a gold chain, but eventually handed it back to the King – who granted him a reward of £50.

The Earl of Montrose was executed for treachery in 1650. After he had been dismembered, his head was fixed on an iron pin on top of Edinburgh's new prison as a deterrent; one hand was set on a city gate at Perth, the other similarly at Stirling; one leg and foot went to Aberdeen, and the other to Glasgow.

When Earl Ferrers was sentenced to death for the murder of one of his servants in 1760, the judge added that his body would then be dissected. Hearing that, the Earl exclaimed 'God forbid!', then quickly changed it to 'God's will be done!'

In the process of erecting a 75ft monument named 'Eternal Life' in Tajikistan in 2004, the scaffolding collapsed, causing the workmen to suffer broken limbs.

In 2004 a drunken driver in the American state of Georgia crashed his truck and the impact beheaded his passenger. The vehicle was still roadworthy so he drove a further twelve miles to his house, leaving the decapitated corpse in the cab, where it was discovered by passers-by the next day.

During excavations in France in 1987, a thighbone was discovered, believed to be that of William the Conqueror.

Following successful battles, Amazonian tribesmen decapitated their enemies and kept the heads as battle trophies; the skins were carefully peeled off, dried and packed with pebbles and sand to give them the necessary shape. Although this custom was discontinued in the 1960s, fake shrunken heads are still sold to tourists as souvenirs.

The severed head of traitor Christopher Layer, which was displayed on Temple Bar in London's Fleet Street for over thirty years, until blown down in a gale in 1753, was found by attorney John Pearce, who showed it to his friends in a nearby tavern before it was buried beneath the hostelry's floor.

By the mid-1800s, a private burial ground in Globe Fields, Mile End, London, which catered for those who could not afford to pay for an expensive funeral, was found to have accommodated as many as 14,000 corpses, deposited in a number of large pits, many of the bodies less than two feet below the surface. In order to make space for as many corpses as possible, the coffins had previously been disposed of by being burned.

When the tomb of William II (1087–1100) in Winchester was opened in 1968, among the many bones was found the flighted shaft of the arrow which reportedly caused his death.

It is believed by many that after a head has been severed by sword or guillotine, the brain lives on for a few seconds. So just as other organs are 'alive' after an accident and can be transplanted, is the brain still capable of thinking? Could the victims therefore have seen the ground coming up to meet them, or the faces of the jeering crowds around the scaffold as their heads were held high?

When the nineteenth-century murderer William Borwick mounted York's scaffold, he said he hoped the rope was strong enough, because, if it broke, he'd fall and be crippled for life!

Between 1640 and 1645 many holy relics of Roman Catholic martyrs burned at the stake were rescued from near the pyre by the servants of the Spanish Ambassador, Count Egmond, and distributed among places of worship in memory of those who had suffered so cruelly. An extensive list of the relics was published in *The Rambler* in 1857. Among many others were those of the priest William Ward, who suffered at London on 26 July 1641: his heart, drawn from the fire in which it had lain for about five hours; the handkerchief he had in his hand when he died; and his diurnal. Of Father Bartholomew Roe: his breviary, a thumb, a piece of burnt lung, a piece of kidney burnt to a cinder and a towel dipped in his blood. Of Mr Arnold Green: a thumb, a piece of burnt liver, a towel dipped in his blood, a nightcap drawn over his eyes when he was hanged, and the apron and sleeves of the executioner. Of the secular priest John Morgan, who perished at London on 26 April 1642: pieces of burnt flesh, some of his hair, four towels dipped in his blood, the straw on which he was laid to be disembowelled, some papers greased with his fat, and the rope with which he had been hanged. Of Francis Bell, who died on the scaffold on 1 December 1643: a right-hand quarter of his body, six pieces of his flesh and fat, three napkins dipped in his blood and melted fat, two fingers and other small bones. And so on, *ad nauseam*.

Shoppers walking along Charing Cross Road in London might be surprised to learn that somewhere under their feet lie the remains of Charles II's favourite Nell Gwynne, together with those of thousands of others. The area was once part of the cemetery of the nearby church of St Martin's-in-the-Fields.

In 2004, occupants of a house in Buckinghamshire were aroused when a burglar broke in. In the ensuing struggle, his false leg was detached. Overpowered by the owners, he was subsequently arrested. In court his defence had hardly a leg to stand on – well, only one.

The sentence of death passed on the Rev. Thomas Hunter on 22 August 1700 for murdering two young children was 'That on the succeeding day he should be executed on a gibbet [gallows] erected for that purpose on the spot where he had committed the murders, but that, previous to the execution, his right hand should be cut off with a hatchet, near the wrist, and then he should be drawn up to the gibbet by a rope [hanged] and when he was dead, hung on chains between Edinburgh and Leith, the knife with which he committed the murder being stuck through his hand, which should be advanced over his head and fixed thereto to the top of the gibbet.'

When Richard II's close friend Robert de Vere died in France, the King had the cadaver returned to England in a perfumed coffin, then opened it and sorrowfully clasped the corpse's hand.

In 2004 workmen found a pyjama-clad skeleton in a Tokyo flat. By the body was a newspaper dated 20 February 1984.

The well-preserved remains of St Francis Xavier, a founder of the Jesuit order, who died in 1552, are displayed to the public every ten years in Goa, and more than three million believers are expected to travel from far and wide to view them.

The Edinburgh *Evening Dispatch* of 28 July 1925 reported a case in Germany involving crematorium attendants who not only stole rings and bracelets from the corpses awaiting cremation, but also snapped off and sold any teeth having gold fillings. They also saved time by burning two corpses at once and then divided the ashes among the two sorrowing families. When all this was discovered, they, like the cadavers they had robbed, were fired.

After the death of Henry V, of Agincourt fame, his bones were cleansed by boiling, and a death mask of leather made of his face and placed on top of his coffin.

In *Reminiscences of Student Days and Dissecting Rooms*, published in 1919, Dr Shepherd related how a student suddenly realised that the corpse purchased from body-snatchers and awaiting anatomising on the table was that of his uncle! 'He was a Frenchman,' the doctor continued, 'and he said to me, "What for you got mine uncle here?" I said I did not know it was his uncle; had I known that, I would never have received him, but if he, the student, was prepared to pay the expense of the corpse's removal, he could have him." The Frenchman thought awhile, then said "S'pose mine uncle come, s'pose he stay" – and he did stay and was properly dissected!'

Henry VI was stabbed to death in the Tower of London in 1471 (the author was not on duty that day!). On his tomb being opened in 1910, *The Times* reported that the authorities found 'human bones lying in no particular order, mixed with the rotting remains of some material in which they had been wrapped. The skull was much broken ... some hair of a brown colour being attached which, in one place, was darker and apparently matted with blood.'

While foundations for machinery were being dug in Fleet Street, London, in 1927, a Roman cemetery was discovered at a depth of eighteen to twenty feet. Row upon row of burial urns, 10 to 15 inches in height, were unearthed, each filled with the calcined bones of long-dead Londoners. Some had been placed there in the first century AD, others in the third century.

In 2003 corpses exhumed in some German cemeteries were found not to have decayed, despite having been buried many years earlier. It was concluded that this could have been due to preservatives in food; or possibly that some coffins used had been made of chipboard, which contains formaldehyde.

Archbishop of Canterbury Simon Sudbury was brutally murdered on Tower Hill during the Peasants' Revolt of 1381. His skull is entombed in the wall of St Gregory's church, Sudbury; his corpse lies buried in Canterbury Cathedral, a ball of lead replacing the head.

Frederick Deeming was executed in 1892 for murdering his wife and burying her beneath the floor of their house in Melbourne, Australia. At the trial it was discovered that while living in England he had also murdered his former wife and their four children, and had disposed of their corpses in the same manner.

A murderer imprisoned in a French gaol in 2004 quarrelled with his cell-mate, smashed the man's head open with an ashtray, then proceeded to scoop out his victim's brains with his hand and eat them.

To stick one's tongue out at people only brings trouble. Witness the case of John Warde and Richard Lyneham, who, in 1380, pretended that they were mutes 'and went about the City carrying an iron hook, pincers, and a piece of leather, in shape like a tongue, with writing around it to the effect *This is the tongue of John Warde*, giving people to understand that their tongues had been pulled out with the said hook, and then cut off with the said pincers; they made a horrible noise like unto a roaring, opening their mouths, where it seemed to all who examined the same, that their tongues had been cut off.' In court they were sentenced to stand in the pillory on three different days, each day for an hour, with the instruments of injury about their necks; after which they were to be returned to Newgate Gaol until orders were given for their release.

The skull of the martyred Venerable Oliver Plunket is revered at Drogheda, Ireland. The flesh and skin, the latter a dark brown colour, are still on the face; parts of the left cheek and the upper lip are burnt black as a result of the fire into which the head was thrown after his execution. A little hair remains in place at the back of the head and there is a deep cut across the crown. The holy relic sometimes emits a perfume which lasts for some minutes after the shrine has been opened.

An Indian man thought little of the occasional stomach twinges he suffered, and it was not until he went into hospital for a minor operation that the surgeons discovered the foetus of his dead twin, which had lain inside him for 36 years.

Above the gateway of the churchyard of St Olave's in Hart Street, East London, are carved stone skulls and crossbones, for within were buried a vast number of victims of the horrific Great Plague of 1665.

Rather than dispose of his finger, which was amputated after being injured in a shooting accident, Prime Minister William Ewart Gladstone had it preserved in formaldehyde and kept it in a safe place until he died in 1898; it was then placed in his coffin prior to his burial in Westminster Abbey.

Instead of throwing away the teeth he had extracted from his patients, Battista Orsenigo, a nineteenth-century dentist, retained them, eventually amassing a collection of over two million molars – quite a stash of gnashers!

Many so-called holy relics are preserved in cathedrals all round the world. Among them are locks of Jesus' mother Mary's hair, part of John the Baptist's skull and the shoulder-blade of Saint Andrew. The mummified penis of Tutankhamun was 'liberated' by an avid collector of such trophies.

A leg bone allegedly of Captain James Cook, taken from his remains after his murder in Hawaii in 1779, was DNA tested in 2004 and proved to be part of either an antler or a seal. It brought about the end of a legend about a leg-end.

It was reported in 2004 that the embalmed corpse of North Korea's Ho Chi Minh lies on display in a glass case in a mausoleum in Hanoi. The hands and face are regularly bathed and the wispy beard is carefully combed. The corpse is visited by thousands of mourners each year.

A leaden drum in the church of Brington is generally supposed to contain the head of Henry Spencer, Earl of Sunderland

(1620–1643), who was fatally wounded at the Battle of Newbury during the Civil War.

French porters working in Parisian dissection rooms made extra francs in the early 1800s by selling human fat, left over from dissections, to local tradesmen, who used it to lubricate the wheels of their delivery wagons. So much spare fat was available that three labourers and a cart drawn by a pair of horses were needed to deliver it to the recipients. It is reported that at the marriage of Napoleon to Maria Louisa, the lamps illuminating the historic ceremony at the Palace of Luxembourg were fuelled by a mixture of melted human fat and more conventional tallow.

When the Scottish leader John Baliol died, his widow had his heart embalmed and placed it in an ivory casket. During the next twenty years she never sat down to meals without the casket being on the table. On her death her instructions were complied with, 'that she be buried with the heart resting on her bosom'.

Louis XVI was guillotined by executioner Charles-Henri Sanson in 1793 during the French Revolution. His son, born in 1785 to Louis and Marie Antoinette, was imprisoned and died of tuberculosis ten years later. The surgeon who performed the postmortem kept the heart as a royal souvenir and, after being owned by many different people during the next two hundred or so years, it was eventually located by the authorities. Following DNA testing, it was placed within a highly ornamented glass egg and, 'resembling a dried mushroom', was buried in 2004 in the royal crypt of Saint-Denis.

Many holy relics survive of the Venerable Nicholas Postgate, found guilty of high treason as a Catholic priest and executed at York on 7 August 1679: part of the rope used to hang him is reportedly at St Mary's Convent, York, while at St Cuthbert's,

Old Elvet, Durham, are two locks of his white hair, his entire jawbone, one of his spinal vertebrae and his right hand.

Corpses disinterred by body-snatchers in the nineteenth century were salted, pickled and sent as specimens to provincial surgical schools in crates bearing innocuous labels. In 1826 no fewer than 28 corpses, belonging to fifteen men, five women, five boys and three girls, were discovered in containers on Liverpool Docks, the ghastly smelling cargo being bound for Leith in Scotland.

The renowned satirist Paul Whitehead died in 1774 and left his heart to his friend Lord le Despencer to be deposited in his mausoleum at West Wycombe. On 16 May 1775, after being wrapped in lead and placed in a marble urn, it was carried to its resting place with unsurpassed ceremony. Preceding the bier bearing the urn 'a grenadier marched in full uniform, nine grenadiers two deep, the odd one last; two German flute players, two surpliced choristers with notes pinned to their backs, two more flute players, eleven singing men in surplices, two French horn players, two bassoon players, six fifers and four drummers with muffled drums. Lord le Despencer, as chief mourner, followed the bier, in his uniform as Colonel of the Bucks Militia, and was followed by nine officers of the same corps, two more fifers, as well as two drummers and twenty soldiers with their firelocks reversed. The Dead March was played, the church bells tolled, and cannons were fired every three and a half minutes. On arrival at the mausoleum, another hour was spent by the procession by going round and round it, singing dirges, after which the urn containing the heart was carried inside and placed on a pedestal bearing Paul Whitehead's name.' But in 1829 someone stole the urn and its whereabouts remain a mystery.

When the House of Commons investigated body-snatching in 1828 it was revealed that one gang of half a dozen body-snatchers dug up no fewer than 312 corpses during one winter, and disposed of them to surgeons as surgical specimens. The cadavers were sold for about £4 4s each, a tax-free total of over £1,300, a veritable fortune in those days.

Many of the remains of soldiers killed in South Africa during the Boer War have been dug up and the bones used by witch doctors in black magic ceremonies and for allegedly curative purposes.

In March 2004 two young boys became the first people since 1899 to be charged with grave-robbing, having broken into the Edinburgh tomb of Sir George 'Bloody' Mackenzie, who, in the seventeenth century, had been the highly unpopular Lord Advocate appointed by Charles II. The youngsters desecrated the body, which they had extracted from the coffin, by cutting the skull off with a knife and using it as a football in the churchyard.

It is estimated that in the vaults and surrounds of St Anne's Church, Soho, 110,240 corpses were interred during 160 years.

Jeremy Bentham died in 1832. As he directed, his body was dissected for the benefit of medical science and his skeleton articulated (the bones wired together in their correct order), suitably padded and dressed, given a head modelled in wax, complete with flowing wig, and seated in an air-tight glass-fronted cabinet in University College, London. In the early 1920s, due to moth damage, the figure was opened up, and Jeremy's skull was found among the stuffing; it now lies, mummified, small, shrivelled and red-coloured, at his feet.

After one of the Gunpowder Plot conspirators, Sir Everard Digby, had been beheaded, the executioner extracted his heart, held it high and shouted, 'This is the heart of a traitor!' – and the head reputedly exclaimed, 'Thou liest!'

A gravedigger admitted to the 1842 Select Committee of the House of Commons that he had witnessed other gravediggers remove handles and fittings from old coffins and sell them, and that they would 'play at what is called skittles, stick up bones in the ground and throw a skull at them as you would a skittle ball.'

FELONIOUS FEMALES

When Hans McFarlane and Helen Blackwood were found guilty of murder and sentenced to be hanged in August 1853, Hans asked the prison governor for permission to marry Helen but was refused. When the couple appeared on the Glasgow scaffold, watched by more than 40,000 spectators, Hans said 'Helen Blackwood, before God and in the presence of these witnesses, I take you to be my wife. Do you consent?' Helen replied, 'I do.' 'Then,' said Hans, 'I declare you to be what you have always been to me, a true and faithful wife, and you die an honest woman.' The clergyman present exclaimed 'Amen!' – then the hangman released the trapdoors.

Margaret Masson was found guilty in Edinburgh in 1806 of killing her husband, but was discovered to be pregnant. After six months she reappeared in court holding her new baby and, in accordance with the law, was sentenced to death and hanged shortly afterwards.

In November 1904 a woman was arrested for drunkenness and confined in police cells, only to be found unconscious the following morning. A doctor pronounced her dead and the body was taken to the nearby Grenoble School of Medicine, where it was duly laid out for the postmortem. But while the surgeon was collecting the necessary instruments, the 'corpse' suddenly sat up and asked for a glass of water! It was later established that the woman was subject to epileptic fits, during which her body assumed a cadaver-like rigidity.

Judy Buenoano was executed in Florida in March 1998 for poisoning her husband. She had previously been sentenced to life imprisonment for drowning her son and also trying to kill her boyfriend with a bomb. Earlier she had murdered her common-law husband using arsenic.

Whenever Bavarian-born Anne-Marie Schneider was present, lights switched themselves on and off, bulbs blew and telephones rang without there being any callers. Although she was investigated at length in the 1960s, no scientific explanations were forthcoming.

On 12 September 1606 Catherine Askew stole a petticoat, a woman's waistcoat and an apron from Agnes Lea. They hanged her.

George I (1660–1727) had two mistresses, one of whom was granted the title of the Countess of Darlington, the other, the Duchess of Kendal. Their figures were such that they were promptly christened by the irreverent courtiers 'the Elephant and the Maypole'.

When Ruth Snyder was executed in 1928, the *New York Daily News* sold 100,000 extra copies of the edition containing the graphic details of her death.

The Halifax Gibbet was a guillotine-like machine used during the seventeenth century. On one occasion, it was reported, a woman riding her horse along Gibbet Street suddenly had a head drop into the basket in front of her.

In 1752 a Dr Smellie urged women who could not breast-feed their babies to employ a wet-nurse, but warned them that employing red-haired women for that purpose wasn't everyone's choice.

Men in Maryland who beat their wives were, until 1952, liable to be sentenced to be whipped themselves.

In court in 1643 the magistrate called for Jane Key to appear before him, but no one responded. The Constable explained that, although she had been sentenced to be whipped from the Bayle to the High Street at the last session, she had fallen and broken her neck. 'But', he went on, 'every morning since, I rubbed her neck with neatsfoot oil and then I whipped her as ordered.'

Due to a tragic miscalculation on the part of the Arizona hangman in February 1930, murderess Eva Dugan was given too long a drop and, as reported by the local newspaper, 'her headless body lay in the pit, ten feet away from the masked head, a pallid chin protruding from the black hood.'

Angelique Tiquet, condemned to death in 1699 for planning the murder of her husband, although she had later relented and stopped the paid killers, knelt on the scaffold and asked the executioner, 'How should I put myself?' Charles Sanson answered, 'With your head up and your hair swept forward over your face.' And, as he swung the heavy sword preparatory to beheading her, Angelique, feminine to the end, exclaimed, 'Be sure not to disfigure me!'

Elizabeth Pinckhard murdered her mother-in-law and was sentenced to death on 27 February 1852. Hangings had always taken place on a Monday and so, when rumours indicated that it would be on 12 March, thousands of people gathered to watch.

When nothing happened at the scaffold site, everyone was bitterly disappointed, and one woman even threatened that she would claim expenses from the sheriff! However, everything turned out fine for execution afficionados on the following day, when ten thousand of them gathered to boo and cheer Mrs Pinckhard as she paid the price for her sins.

Between 1753 and 1878, 36 women were executed in Scotland, 29 of them for murder.

Mrs Anne Turner, guilty of supplying the poison which killed Sir Thomas Overbury, was hanged at Tyburn in November 1615. She was reputedly the inventor of yellow starch, and wore a 'Cobweb Lawn Ruff of that colour' on the scaffold. Yellow starch immediately went out of fashion.

Similarly, when double poisoner Mrs Jaffray appeared on the Glasgow gallows in May 1838 she wore a Rob Roy tartan shawl wrapped around her shoulders. That garment also went out of fashion, and it was some years before it appeared on the Scottish catwalks again.

Joan Rogers was indicted for highway robbery in July 1610 for assaulting Mary Palmer and stealing a hat. She was sentenced to death.

The seventeenth-century Judge Jeffries, not noted for his mercy or consideration for the fair sex, once sentenced a woman to be punished by exclaiming, 'Hangman, I charge you to pay particular attention to the lady! Scourge her till her blood runs down – it is Christmas, a cold time for Madam to strip. See that you warm her shoulders thoroughly!' Readers will be pleased to know that Jeffries ended his days dying in the Bloody Tower of the Tower of London while awaiting trial himself.

When there was a great need for women in the early male-dominated colonies of America in the mid-1700s, six thousand of them sailed in 1746, and a further ten thousand were waiting for sea passages.

As late as 1783 a woman was burned at the stake in Ipswich for murdering her husband.

Thomasina Saro was hanged in Montreal's Bordeaux Gaol in March 1935 for murdering her husband. The hangman miscalculated her weight and the excessively long drop nearly severed her head.

Between 1934 and 1951 Rhoda Martin poisoned not only her mother but three of her children and her second and fourth husbands. She was executed in Montgomery, Alabama, on 11 October 1957.

Murderess Mary Timney, in a state of collapse, had to be carried on to the Dumfries scaffold; as she stood on the drop, supported by a wardress on each side of her, the hangman reached for the lever, but was abruptly halted by the Sheriff, who assumed that the envelope suddenly handed up to him contained a last-minute reprieve. However, it was only a request from a London newspaper editor for a description of how Mary had died, so the ghastly farrago restarted – and the trapdoors fell.

Isabella Condon, guilty of forging counterfeit coins, was taken to Tyburn together with three robbers on 22 June 1768. The men were hanged but Isabella was fastened to a stake, the faggots about her set alight, and her body consumed to ashes. London newspapers reported 'that she had cried bitterly and declared that the last part of her sentence she had to undergo, affected her beyond every other consideration'.

Captured after the Jacobite Rebellion of 1715, the Earl of Nithsdale was sentenced to death and incarcerated in the Tower of London but escaped, walking out dressed as a woman, his cheeks rouged, his beard concealed by a scarf, thanks to the ingenuity of his wife who visited him daily and had smuggled the necessary accessories past the guards.

In Bahrain in 2004 a woman disguised herself with a beard and donned a robe, in an attempt to lead the prayers in a mosque, a practice forbidden to women under Islamic laws. She was prevented by guards from committing such a sacrilegious act.

Canadian Antonia Sprecage was hanged in 1919 but, having been given too short a drop, was strangled, and did not die until an hour and ten minutes had elapsed.

As her last meal Frau Zillmann, guilty of murdering her brutal husband, chose a well-done beefsteak and coffee, saying, 'I should like to eat as much as I like, just once more,' before being led out to the scaffold, her dress cut out at her neck to her shoulders. And in that year of 1893, in Germany, she was beheaded by the axe.

In March 1722 Catherine McCulloch was secured to Stirling's market cross and, having been found guilty of eavesdropping, had her ear severed by the hangman.

Clemence Carter was found guilty of murdering her daughter in May 1617 by giving her two pieces of 'green coporis', from which she died. She claimed to be pregnant, but a Jury of Matrons, twelve in number, examined her and found her not to be, and so she was hanged.

Highwaymen, yes – but highwaywomen? When, in 1763, one of each gender held up a couple in Harrow, the female member of the pair 'insisted that the gentleman should do her a good turn under the hedge', whereupon her male colleague followed suit with the gentleman's lady friend (thereby giving an entirely new meaning to the word 'waylaid'!)

The last case of legal drowning took place in 1697 when a woman guilty of theft was sentenced in Scotland to be drowned in the Loch of Spyne. When, early in the nineteenth century, the loch was drained, the skeleton of the unfortunate woman appeared as the water level dropped, identified by a ring on one of her fleshless fingers.

Six women were hanged at Newgate between 1846 and 1896: Martha Browning for murdering an old woman for a five pound note, Harriet Parker for killing her lover's two children after he deserted her, Catherine Wilson for secretly poisoning Mrs Soames, Frances Stewart for throwing her grandchild into the River Thames, Eleanor Wheeler for the Kentish Town murder, and Annie Dyer, 'baby farmer', who murdered two infants and probably many more.

Rarely has a woman been racked in this country; more rarely still has she subsequently been burned at the stake, yet that was the fate suffered by Lady Jane Douglas in 1535. Accused by a vengeful William Lyons, whose advances she had rebuffed, of conspiring to poison James V of Scotland, she was stretched on the rack until, unable to endure the appalling agony, she confessed. Although no other proof existed of her guilt, she was tied to a stake surrounded by tar barrels on Castle Hill, Edinburgh, and burned to death.

In the 1600s, when to have the 'wrong' religion was a serious crime, widow Elizabeth Wager was remanded to the Grand Jury because she 'harboured recusants [Roman Catholics who did not attend Church of England services as was required by law] who had been seen going into her house by night, with the intent to infect and poison many of His Majesty's subjects with dregs of popery.'

An eighteenth-century equivalent of good guides to London's restaurants, theatres, etc. was *Harris' List of Covent Garden Ladies* which promised 'an exact Description of the most celebrated Ladies of Pleasure', price 2s 6d (the cost of the guidebook, not the Ladies!).

Like Elizabeth Wager, Dorothy Browne was remanded to the Grand Jury, but for a very different reason. The court was told in 1620 that 'she had not scoured the watercourse on her backside, with the result that much of the street is a very stinking puddle and fit to breed infection by reason of the filthy savours that arise from it.'

Elizabeth Barton, known as the 'Holy Maid of Kent', forecast that if Henry VIII went ahead and divorced Catherine of Aragon, he would die the death of a villain. Not the most tactful thing to say to Henry, who promptly had her hanged and decapitated, further ordering that her head be displayed on London Bridge – the only female head to be exhibited thereon.

Would-be assassin Margaret Nicholson was confined in a lunatic asylum after she tried to stab George III in August 1784. She was seized by his escort and would have been roughly handled by the crowd had not His Majesty intervened, saying 'The poor creature is mad; do not hurt her, she has not hurt me.'

Deserted by her lover, Manette Bonhourt became a mass murderer, ensnaring men, drugging them and killing them with hammer blows. A gorgeous blonde, she disposed of nearly twenty men who were unable to resist her charms – or the hammer. Even Henri Sanson, the executioner, stared admiringly at her as, on the Paris scaffold on 16 May 1808, she smiled at him and murmured provocatively, 'Don't you think it a pity to cut off a head as beautiful as mine?'

Just as Rose Stinnette was being executed in South Carolina's electric chair in January 1947 a fuse blew, and, although the current being transmitted to the chair was unaffected, the execution chamber was thrown into darkness and the only illumination was the sparks coming from Rose's head and arms.

NOOSE-KNOTTERS AND SLICERS

In 1951 Viscount Templewood stated that 'Executions are so much a part of British history that it is almost impossible for many excellent people to think of the future without them.'

As reported in *St James' Gazette* of 8 August 1893, the method of judicial execution in Austria was strangulation, accomplished partly by the rope and partly by the compression of the felon's windpipe by the executioner. This process sometimes took as long as five minutes before the victim was declared dead.

William Calcraft holds the record of being hangman for 45 years, from 1829 to 1874.

When a vacancy for the post of English hangman arose in 1883, 1,400 people applied for the job.

The Canadian executioner during the 1930s was Arthur Bartholomew English, who performed or assisted at more than six hundred executions.

Tom Cheshire, deputy hangman from 1808 to 1840, once boasted that he had assisted in the hanging of about five hundred and fifty felons 'and never had a haccident 'cos I allers carry a good rope'.

William Brunskill, lord of the scaffold from 1786 to 1814, made his debut somewhat theatrically. Having pulled the lever and sent seven malefactors plunging simultaneously to their doom, he advanced to the edge of the boards, placed one hand on his breast and made a low sweeping bow.

Executions were usually carried out on a weekday, but an exception was made in 1558 when, as recorded by John Stow, 'The first of September, it being a Sonday, one Cratwell, Hangman of London, and two other, were hanged at the wrestling ground by Clerkenwell, for robbing a booth at Bartholomew Faire.'

At the turn of the last century the method by which the electric chair was controlled was usually effective if primitive. The executioner communicated with the operator of the electricity generator elsewhere in the building or the prison grounds by means of five bell signals. The first signal was sounded a quarter of an hour or so early, to warn the operator to start the machine; once the victim had been strapped securely into the chair and the electrodes attached to his or her head and leg, the second bell resulted in the current flowing into the victim's body. A third bell called for more current if necessary; a fourth would bring a reduction of the current, and the fifth would switch the generator off. No bells were tolled for the victim.

Six generations of the Sanson dynasty of executioners dominated the Paris scaffold for 159 years.

Edward Hand was due to receive eighty strokes of the whip in Glasgow in 1822; twenty at the gaol, twenty in Stockwell Street, twenty in Glassford Street and twenty at the Cross. The punishment was delayed by an argument over who was to tie him to the back of the cart, the sheriff or the hangman, and who should carry the standby cat-o-nine-tails. After some time the matter was resolved, Hand was thoroughly whipped and the crowds were satisfied with the entertainment.

When the Earl of Essex was beheaded in 1601, the executioner was one Derrick, whose life he had saved years before, after Derrick had been condemned to death for raping a woman in Calais. One good turn? Hardly!

The nineteenth-century Indian executioner Mishrilal Mullick occasionally officiated at ten or even twenty hangings a day; his son hanged six hundred victims over a fifty-year period; and *his* son Nata, although he had not performed an execution for 15 years, revived all his skills when hanging a murderous rapist in August 2004, afterwards praying for the man's soul in a nearby temple.

William Billington, Bolton's hangman in the early 1900s, served a short prison sentence himself in 1905 for not maintaining his wife and family.

In bygone days the hangman of Wigtown in Scotland had to be a condemned man himself, reprieved from his own execution to carry out others, until he was too old; then he would be hanged. If he died in harness, the town would lose the honour of having its own hangman. But the last man to hold that post was so well-liked that, when he fell ill, his friends propped him up in bed, surrounded by the tools of his trade – he was a shoemaker – and fooled the town officials, so that instead of being hanged, he was allowed to pass away quietly. Wigtown subsequently had to share a hangman with other towns.

Until capital punishment was abolished in England, the wording of the death sentence, as decided in 1903, was 'The sentence of the Court upon you is that you be taken from this place to a lawful prison and thence to a place of execution, and that you be there hanged by the neck until you be dead; and that your body be afterwards buried within the precincts of the prison in which you shall have been confined before your execution. And may the Lord have mercy on your soul.'

James Botting, an early nineteenth-century hangman, was once jeered at by a group of ne'er-do-wells in the street. When asked why he didn't retaliate he replied drily, 'I never quarrel with my customers!' As it happened, one of the group later turned to crime and did become a customer on the scaffold, where Botting hanged him on 12 April 1817.

When one of his victims, about to be drowned instead of being guillotined, asked French Revolutionary Representative Carrier for a glass of water, he replied brutally, 'No need! In a few minutes you will be drinking out of the big cup!'

Assistant hangman Allen didn't move quickly enough in 1928, and, when his boss Robert Baxter pulled the lever, fell through the drop with the condemned man.

To avoid retribution by the condemned man's friends and relatives, nineteenth-century Scottish hangmen disguised themselves on the scaffold by wearing black masks, black cloaks and sometimes even black wigs.

Hangmen had to be legally authorised before carrying out their duties, in order to absolve them of a charge of murder, and so were given a formal written notification by the appropriate Sheriff, which stated that 'I, John Smith, of ....
in the county of ...., sheriff of the said county of ...., do hereby authorise you to hang Tom Robinson who now lies under sentence of death in Her Majesty's

prison at ....' The certificate was then signed and dated.

The ashes of the high-ranking war criminals hanged by John C. Woods after World War II were dumped in an Army garbage can and thrown into the River Isar near Munich by four American Army generals.

Richard Brandon, believed to be the executioner who decapitated Charles I, is said to have qualified for the post of public hangman as a young boy, by beheading cats and dogs.

During his years as executioner, the American Robert G. Elliott, who died on 10 October 1939, executed 387 men and women in the electric chair.

During hangman Thomas Askern's last execution in 1877, the rope broke and the condemned man fell heavily into the pit, dying later.

In the 1920s, executioners in the USA were paid a fee of $150 for each execution carried out.

Archibald Hare took a long time to die on the scaffold in October 1851; he dropped a mere two feet into the pit, then spun round like a top, clutching at the rope desperately in an effort to relieve the strangulation, and it wasn't until Murdoch, the Scottish hangman, added his own weight to that of the victim's by swinging from the man's legs that Hare paid the price for his crimes.

John Thrift, hangman from 1735 to 1752, was buried in St Paul's Churchyard, Covent Garden. All traces of his and other graves were lost when the cemetery was later paved over and the area became a popular tourist attraction.

When Ruth Snyder was found guilty of murdering her husband in 1927, rumours abounded that the official executioner was reluctant to despatch a woman. Many applied for the job of executing her, one woman writing, 'I saw in the news that you just did not care to execute Mrs Snyder. If you don't want to do it, will you let me have first offer? I won't mind it one bit to execute Mrs Snyder. It is just what she should get, the electric chair. I could execute Mrs Snyder with a good heart and think I had done a good deed. I think if they did have a woman executioner, it would be no more than right to have a woman to execute a woman, and that would take a whole lot off your mind. If you would like to have me help you the night she is put in the chair, I would be more than glad to do so. I hope to hear from you soon.' The offer was of course ignored.

In 1739 William Jackson, awaiting execution in Newgate Prison, saw the blacksmith enter his cell carrying a tape measure with which to measure him for the 'suit of irons' that would contain his corpse when it was suspended on the gibbet – and dropped down dead with fright.

The English executioner James Billington hanged 147 criminals between 1884 and 1901.

Before going to the guillotine, victims had to have their hair cropped short at the back by the assistant executioner Henri Sanson, for obvious reasons. On approaching M. de Laroque with scissors at the ready, however, Sanson stopped short when his victim remarked, 'I'll save you the trouble!' and calmly removed the wig which covered his bald head.

At the executions of Lords Balmarino and Kilmarnock for treason in 1746, executioner John Thrift, dressed in white on the black-draped scaffold, was overcome by nerves, fainted and had to be revived with a glass of wine before beheading Lord Kilmarnock. After fresh sawdust had been spread over the boards and he had donned a clean white suit, he decapitated Lord Balmerino, although it took him three blows with the axe to sever his victim's head.

In an interview he gave in 1912, Radclive, the Canadian hangman, stated that he had carried out 132 executions.

Anatole Deibler, France's last executioner, guillotined 395 criminals. The fourteen diaries in which he recorded every detail of each beheading, covering the period 1890–1939, were sold at auction in Paris in 1991.

Forty-eight doctors and guards, who had been in charge of the infamous concentration camp at Mauthausen, where thousands of prisoners were brutally put to death during World War II, were hanged during two days in May 1947 by US Army hangmen.

Two men were due to be executed on 25 March 1723, but the hangman was drunk and, mistakenly believing that he had three clients to despatch, attempted to put a noose round the neck of the parson standing on the scaffold. It was with much difficulty that he was prevented from doing so by the gaoler.

Hangman James Botting retired early in the nineteenth century after suffering a stroke. Confined to his bed, he had hallucinations of the 175 felons he had executed, describing how they paraded around the bedroom with their heads, swathed in the traditional white caps, tilted to one side as if still suspended on the rope. 'Damn their eyes!' he used to complain indignantly, 'if only they'd hold their heads up and take off their caps, I wouldn't care a damn about any of them!'

Fifty-three Japanese war criminals were executed by firing squad in the Philippines and Japan after World War II by Lieutenant Charles Rexroad and his men.

On 5 June 1797 hangman Brunskill and his assistant noosed two criminals on the scaffold, but just as a clergyman and a priest were praying with the felons the trap accidentally opened and all six men hurtled into the depths. The felons died as their ropes tightened, while the other four landed in a struggling heap at the bottom of the pit, oaths coming from at least two of them.

Whenever a doomed criminal appeared on the scaffold, the crowd would shout, 'Hats off! Hats off!' – not, as may be thought, as a sign of respect for the man about to die a horrible death, but so that the spectators' view wouldn't be obscured.

The French executioner Jean-Baptiste Sanson had seven sons and, as that profession was a family tradition, all of them served accordingly; one became Monsieur de Paris when his father suffered paralysis, while the others served at Etampes, Montpellier, Meaux, Soissons, Orleans and Rheims. At family feasts they would address each other formally, saying, 'Are you thinking of ordering one of the newly designed guillotines, Monsieur de Rheims?' and 'Did that murderer Georges de Blum give you much trouble last week, Monsieur de Soissons?'

When, in 1939, following the death of the American executioner Elliott, the vacant post was advertised, ten thousand people applied, more than two thousand of them being women.

Andrew Boyle, Edinburgh hangman in the 1700s, was arrested for theft but escaped dressed in women's clothes; he was caught later and transported to the colonies for life.

EXCRUCIATING EQUIPMENT

A gallows large enough to accommodate twenty felons at a time was constructed on the orders of Arkansas Judge Isaac C. Parker in 1875 to bring law and order to the state. He convicted nine thousand criminals in 21 years. In one case, a man found guilty of killing a man for his boots was hanged wearing them.

Hanging, it is said, was invented by the first person who discovered that a rope tied round a man's neck is held in place by the projecting mass of his head.

Interrogation during the Spanish Inquisition included being questioned while being tortured with a tourniquet type of instrument, usually placed around the arm or the thigh, the screw being tightened to compress the flow of blood through the main artery. The answers of the 'heretic' were recorded under the headings 'First-Turn', 'Second-Turn' and so on. The members of the tribunal would decide whether the victim should be admitted into the Church as a penitent or be punished by being burned to death.

State Papers of 1583 contain a statement issued by Elizabeth I's minister Lord Burghley: 'The Queen's servants, the Warders [of the Tower of London], whose office and act it is to handle the rack, were ever by those that attended the examinations, *specially charged to use it in as charitable manner as such a thing might be!*' (author's italics).

In earlier centuries in Asia, suspects were given dry rice to eat; those who couldn't swallow it all were adjudged guilty, based on the belief that human emotions affect the workings of the salivary glands.

During the French Revolution, between 14 July 1789 and 21 October 1796, 370 women were beheaded by the Paris guillotine, and 2,548 men.

The effect on the body during an execution by the electric chair is such that its initial shock destroys the nervous system instantaneously, paralysing the brain before the victim is aware of the onset of the pain. It has been estimated that unconsciousness then ensues within one two-hundred-and-fortieth of a second.

An eye-watering device adopted by the Spaniards was known as the 'Spanish Donkey', an inverted V-shaped wooden structure about six feet in height. The victim was positioned astride it and weights attached to his ankles. The inevitable and ghastly results are left to the reader's imagination.

In addition to hanging felons, nineteenth-century English hangmen also had to inflict lesser punishments on juvenile miscreants, such as flogging them, either with four-foot-long birch rods plaited together or with the nine-thonged whip, the dreaded cat-o'-nine-tails. For this task the hangman received a bonus of 10s a week plus 2s 6d for each flogging administered.

To persuade Allan Stewart to renounce his claim to a certain property in the seventeenth century, the Earl of Cassilis had him tied to a spit in the dungeon of Dunure Castle near Ayr; a roasting fire was lighted beneath him and, while some men-at-arms slowly rotated the spit, others basted him with cooking oil. It worked.

An Irish priest named Hurley was, in 1583, accused of treason and, when the Irish Government asked what measures to take, London suggested the rack. But the Irish didn't have one, so Queen Elizabeth's Secretary of State, Walsingham, never short of ideas, proposed that 'Hurley's feet should be toasted against the fire wearing hot [iron] boots'. Irish tradition says that melted resin (as used in varnishes) was actually poured into the boots. This produced the required confession, which, true or false, was enough to have him executed.

The drop trapdoor of the Delaware gallows in 1935 was operated not by a lever, as was the general practice, but by a bolt withdrawn at the vital moment by a forty-foot-long rope, which was pulled by the hangman stationed some distance away from the scaffold.

In some Eastern countries those suspected of committing a crime were told they would by 'tried' by a magic donkey. They were then sent, one at a time, into a darkened room and told to pull the 'animal's' tail, the magistrate having informed them that if they were guilty, the animal would bray loudly. The tail was covered in soot, so suspects afterwards found to have clean hands, because they had never touched the tail, were assumed to be guilty.

In order to induce the young Princess Victoria to hold her head high, her mother tied a holly twig under her chin.

In 1577 Thomas Sherwood was incarcerated in a Tower cell which was below high-water mark and without any lighting. The water flowed in and out with the tide, bringing with it rats, which during his fitful sleep tore the flesh from his arms and legs. His suffering didn't last long, for he was eventually executed for high treason.

Torture was never legal in England, even under the Tudors, but it could still be administered if the ban were set aside by the Privy Council, a group who met in the Star Chamber at Westminster to decide if it was really necessary – as indeed they did, in many cases.

An obdurate Chinese witness could be persuaded to give evidence by being flogged in a peculiarly cruel manner. Lying face down, he would be whipped on the backs of his thighs, the executioner striking them with the concave side of a split bamboo, the edges of which quickly cut deep into the flesh.

Few people in mediaeval Germany would hesitate to confess to anything, true or not, were they subjected to torture by the Skull Crusher, which consisted of a metal cap positioned on the top of the head and attached by metal straps to a plate fitted under the victim's chin. The two sections were then slowly screwed together, forcing the victim's teeth out of his jaws. Further persuasion was applied by the executioner tapping the metal cap and sending surges of agonising pain through the sufferer's entire body.

A nineteenth-century 'community' instrument of punishment consisted of clips secured tightly to the victim's nose, painfully restricting the breathing for a specified number of hours.

Many instruments of torture were given female names, doubtless for psychological reasons, such as the 'Scottish Maiden', a guillotine-type machine; the 'Nuremberg Maiden', a hollow, spike-lined figure; and the 'Duke of Exeter's Daughter', the Tower's rack. In mediaeval Germany, interrogators employed 'stretching gallows', a vertical rack; at its base were iron rings through which the victim's feet were secured, while his hands were tied to a triangle above his head and elevated by means of ropes and pulleys. This machine was affectionately called 'Schlimme Liesel', 'Fearful Eliza'.

In order to administer torture, the criminal had first to be caught, and this was achieved by using a 'Thief-catcher'. One German model consisted of a long iron shaft terminating at the top in two semi-circular jaws which, when closed, formed a hoop. Sharp triangular spikes lined the hoop and, when it was pushed against the neck or waist of the thief, the spring-operated jaws opened and closed, imprisoning the felon while keeping him at a safe distance from his captor.

One incredibly brave man was the Rev. Edward Peacham, who, in 1614, was accused of criticising the conduct of government officials and the King for his extravagance. To make him confess his treachery he was first put in manacles, suspended by his wrists, his feet clear of the floor, for many hours. When he remained silent, further efforts were made to encourage him to plead guilty: as Secretary of State Wenwood wrote, 'Peacham was this day examined before torture, in torture, between torture, and after torture; notwithstanding nothing could be drawn from him.' Sent to prison in Taunton, he died of gaol fever, typhus, two years later.

In the method of execution known as being 'Broken on the Wheel', the victim was tied spreadeagled on a horizontal cartwheel, then had each limb shattered in two places with an iron bar, and was finally dispatched with a blow to the chest. The practice was abolished in France in 1788.

Anne Boleyn's eyes and lips were seen to continue moving after she had been beheaded, and it has since been calculated that oxygen can remain in the brain for up to seven seconds after the spinal cord has been severed.

What's in a name! In the days when Tyburn gallows held sway – in more ways than one – London's Park Lane was known as Tyburn Lane, and Oxford Street was Tyburn Road.

An account exists of an early guillotine used in Italy in 1702, consisting of two uprights and a blade weighted with a hundred pounds of lead, released when a cord was severed. The condemned man was guided by a 'penitent' to kneel over the block and hold his head still. Following prayers, the executioner cut the cord and the blade fell, leaving the severed head in the penitent's hands. The momentum of the blade was such that it buried itself two inches in the block after passing through the victim's neck.

Until 1751 Tyburn gallows consisted of two posts and a cross-piece, but it was then updated, its suspension capacity being increased by the addition of a third post and two more cross-pieces. The first victim to launch, or rather be launched, by the Triple Tree was a fervent Roman Catholic, Dr John Store, who was hanged and quartered. It was reported that 'the executioner slit open his stomach and while he was rifling through his bowels, the doctor sat up and dealt him a blow.'

Chastity belts were devices to lock around a female waist to prevent all except the husband, who had a key, from being overly intimate with the lady. They were still being manufactured in France as recently as 1910.

In the Middle Ages, Catholics in the Low Countries were tortured by the Protestants by having a bowl containing a few rats strapped, open-end down, on to their bare stomachs. Glowing coals were then placed on the bottom of the container, the heat being of such intensity that there was but one way out for the rodents. . . .

In the twelfth century confessions were extracted by making suspects undergo the Ordeal by Fire. This entailed walking barefoot over a number of red-hot ploughshares, or carrying red-hot irons in the hands. If the wounds had not healed after three days, they would be deemed guilty.

It was alleged that the guillotine used to behead Louis XVI was later shipped to French Guiana and used to execute convicts in the penal colony there.

Vietnamese firing squads were reported in 2004 to be so inaccurate that they only managed to inflict flesh-wounds on the victims. The authorities were considering replacing them with a method using a computerised system of firing a weapon remotely, or by lethal injection.

In early centuries gallows dotted the countryside, giving rise to an anecdote about a shipwrecked sailor who, on scrambling ashore and seeing the ghastly structures, fell on his knees and thanked Providence that he had landed in a Christian country!

When the church of St Martin in Bishopsgate was demolished in 1874 the authorities reported that 'among the contents of the vaults were the remains of a Mrs Abigail Vaughan, who left a legacy of four shillings per annum to purchase faggots (firewood) for the burning of heretics.'

The very first guillotine was made in the Cour du Commerce, Rue Saint-André-des-Arts. In about 1900 its base was discovered, on which the scaffold had been erected when trials were made, using live sheep.

Thomas Gunvyll and John Allen used a forged letter to gain money from Thomas Petchey and, found guilty, were sentenced to be publicly pilloried at Colchester, with a paper on their heads reading 'for getting money by a counterfeit letter' and then to be imprisoned until they repaid Petchey the £36 10s they had obtained.

The earliest English method of hanging using a drop consisted of a small platform raised a few inches above the level of the surrounding boards, but when it fell it occasionally left the victim standing on tiptoe, choking. Later mechanisms consisted of a single trapdoor hinged to one side of the hole, which tended to swing the victim off-centre instead of falling straight down. Eventually the double trap-door proved to be the most effective, although, to prevent them rebounding and trapping the descending victim between them, or, even worse, catapulting him back up again, spring clips were fitted on the side walls of the drop which caught corresponding catches on the underside of the doors, thereby locking them back after opening.

In the original design of the French guillotine, the blade was cres-cent-shaped, but Louis XVI suggested that it would cut better if it were triangular. It would – and it did, nine months later, when the King himself was decapitated by it.

Being broken on the wheel in France was not restricted to males; to mention but a few, Marie Picard was executed in that manner on December 1772 for robbery and murder, Edme Brochart on 14 January 1775, and Charlotte Beuton on 16 May 1775.

The assumption that the ball and chain was purely a medieval method of restraint is not entirely correct; in some American gaols a heavy iron ankle cuff, known as an 'Oregon Boot', serves the same purpose.

Cayenne pepper was used in 1856 in Pentonville Prison, London, to subdue a violent prisoner; it was burnt outside the door and the smoke blown into his cell.

Before being used to decapitate live victims, the French guillotine was taken to a Paris hospital and tried out on several dead bodies. It was successful.

When, late in the nineteenth century, English executioner William Marwood devised the Drop Table, based on the victim's weight, muscular development and similar factors, to decide on the length of drop in feet and inches, the old method of attaching the rope to a hook was replaced by tying it to a short length of chain secured to the beam; accurate adjustments were then made by adding or removing links as necessary.

When executions in public were discontinued in 1868, new rules specified that: they should take place at 8 a.m. on the first day after the intervention of three Sundays from the day on which sentence is passed; a black flag should be hoisted at the moment of execution upon a flagstaff mounted on a conspicuous part of the prison, and displayed for one hour; the bell of the prison, or that of a neighbouring church, should be tolled for fifteen minutes before and after the execution; and the certificate of death should be exhibited for 24 hours near the principal entrance to the prison.

When Tamerlane the Great (1335–1405) caught Bajazet, Emperor of the Turks, he had him enclosed in an iron cage, which was carried everywhere the conqueror went for three years, until at last, despairing of ever being released, Bajazet struck his head with such violence that he died.

A 'San Quentin Overcoat' is a highly constricting type of strait-jacket used in some prisons in the USA.

At Wandsworth Prison, London, a shed standing some little distance from the main buildings was used as the execution chamber, referred to callously as the 'meat shed'. Nearby was a narrow area of turf and, in the wall bounding it, square stone slabs were inset at intervals, each denoting the burial place of an executed man.

Most electric chairs are made of heavy wood, standing on a rubber mat and bolted to the floor. They have wide arms, and their high backs, incorporating adjustable padded headrests, are tilted slightly. The chairs have three legs, two at the rear and a wide one at the front fitted with ankle grips. Eight leather straps secure the victim's wrists and ankles, upper arms, chest and abdomen. Two under-floor cables conduct the current, one to the electrodes in the headpiece, the other to the leg electrode. The controls are situated nearby so that the executioner can regulate the flow of current depending on the rate of demise of the victim.

In 1730 forger Japhet Crook was sentenced not only to have all his land and house forfeited to the court but also to stand in the pillory for an hour; then his ears were to be cut off, and his nose slit and seared with a hot iron.

In 1783 the London execution site was moved from Tyburn to a new location immediately outside the walls of Newgate Prison; the Tyburn gallows were then sold and converted into stands for beer barrels in the cellars of a nearby public house. ('I'll never drink another drop!')

In France, execution by drowning continued to be used for some cases as late as 1793.

The guillotine was adopted because the French Revolutionary Council decided that, instead of being hanged, ordinary criminals should be executed by the more 'honourable' way of being beheaded by the sword, like members of the upper classes when killed on the field of battle. But when executioner Sanson pointed out that, because a sword blade is blunted after one use, thousands of execution swords would be needed, the guillotine blade was the obvious alternative. When hundreds of aristocrats had later to be 'exterminated', the guillotine became the essential tool for the decapitation production line.

From the early nineteenth century, the drop trapdoors on English and Scottish scaffolds were bridged by two planks on which the warders stood while gripping the victim's bound arms; with their free hands they held on to ropes suspended from the beam above them.

Early in the twentieth century chloride of lime was used in Folsom Penitentiary to quell mutinous inmates; the cell floor was soaked with dampened lime and the prisoner not removed from the cell until the biting fumes had convinced him of the futility of further protests.

In one common method of hanging in America, the rope passed over pulleys, a weight on the other end balancing that of the victim; he stood on a small trapdoor, his weight releasing a quantity of buckshot which rolled down a slope until it released the trigger retaining the main weight. The method was eventually abandoned as being more like suicide than execution.

The early French guillotines were subsequently improved, some having a hole through which the headless bodies fell into a wheeled container for later transfer to the cemetery. Another invention, which involved three blades but only one release, thereby tripling decapitation output, was rejected.

WHAT A WAY TO GO!

George, Duke of Clarence, was reportedly drowned in a barrel of rich heady Malmsey wine in the Tower of London in 1478; there is no truth in the rumour that he got out of it three times to visit the toilet.

American executioner Robert G. Elliott, in his book *Agent of Death*, describes what happens when the current of the electric chair is switched on. 'The figure in the chair pitches forward, straining against the straps. There is the whining cry of the current and a crackling, sizzling sound. The body turns a vivid red. Sparks often fly from the electrodes. A wisp of white or dull grey smoke may rise from the top of the head or the leg to which the electrode is attached; this is produced by the drying out of the sponge lining the electrode. The hair is also singed and, despite every effort to prevent it, sometimes the flesh is burned. An offensive odour is generally present.'

When Henry Malanik was hanged – the last man to be executed in the Province of Manitoba – the noose tore his jugular vein open, drenching the walls with blood as his cadaver swung from side to side in the pit.

A Sunday paper described the prolonged end of the Russian Tsarina's favourite Rasputin, brought about by Prince Yussoupov and his colleagues, who, having failed to poison him with vast amounts of cyanide and shooting him in the head, finally resorted to tying him up and throwing him in the river Niva. He died.

The fourteenth-century conqueror Tamerlane, self-proclaimed 'Scourge of God', used a weapon known as Greek Fire, incendiary jelly fired from bronze tubes. He was responsible for the slaughter of 90,000 residents of Baghdad, and used their skulls as bricks with which to build scores of towers.

With effect from 1752 judges were empowered to order that after execution a criminal's corpse be hanged in chains, the order to include the terrible words: 'where you shall be hung until the fowls of the air pick your flesh off your body, and your bones bleach and whiten in the winds of heaven, thereby to afford a constant warning of the fatal consequences which almost invariably attend the indulgence of the passions.'

Although he was already dead, Cromwell's body was disinterred at the Restoration of the Monarchy and decapitated by the axe; it took eight strokes to sever the head.

It was reported in a local paper on 1 July 1813 that 'the Jubilee coach, having just left Halifax for Leeds, had an accident which caused the death of three people. The driver and several others had broken limbs. The vehicle was a new one and had commenced running the day before.' No mention was made of a manufacturer's warranty.

When John Brown (whose body 'lies a-mouldering in his grave') attacked Harper's Ferry in 1859 he was armed with the sword presented by Frederick the Great to George Washington, which had been stolen from Washington's nephew that day. It didn't help him, for he was later hanged.

During the enactment of a burning-at-the-stake scene during the 2002 filming of an episode in the reign of Mary Tudor, a sudden gust of wind blew the flames across the face of the actor playing the part of the 'heretic' Archbishop Cranmer; fortunately he was rescued in time and suffered only minor burns.

For killing Thomas Peirson, rector of Ilford, in December 1617, William Hilles was sentenced to be hanged near the place of the murder, and then to be suspended there in chains.

Determined to commit suicide, a Taiwanese man leapt from the top of a 23-storey office block in 2004, but survived – which is more than can be said for the woman in the car on which he landed: he broke his legs, but she was killed outright.

When the judge at the trial of felon Jerry Abershaw sentenced him to death by donning the black cap, Abershaw did likewise with his own hat; he also died on the scaffold gripping a flower between his teeth!

After murderer William Burke, of Burke and Hare, had been hanged in Edinburgh in 1829 his corpse was exhibited in Surgeons' Hall. Twenty-four thousand people queued up to walk slowly past the operating table and inspect it.

As a sedative before being hanged, morphine was given to killer Joseph-Pierre Richard, executed in December 1957 for murdering a teenaged girl, Kay de la Perelle, in New Brunswick, Canada.

Gibbetting – being encased in a suit consisting of strips of iron and suspended from a gibbet resembling a tall sign-post – was the fate of one John Whitfield in the 1700s. The only difference from the usual practice was that he was still alive. He didn't suffer for very long, however, for a passing coachman felt sorry for him and shot him.

When Ciro Annichiarico, a Calabrian outlaw, faced a firing squad in 1817, so inaccurate were the members of the squad that even after being struck by a fusillade of 21 bullets he was only wounded. The twenty-second killed him.

In pre-DNA days, the best way to avoid leaving clues at the scene of one's crime was to strip naked before committing it. This was the technique adopted by the French valet Courvoisier in 1840 when he slew his employer, Lord Russell. However, he was fully clothed, complete with hempen collar, when he kept an appointment with executioner William Calcraft on the scaffold. His death mask was later exhibited in Mme Tussaud's Chamber of Horrors.

So powerfully built was the Canadian murderer Earl Lund, hanged in 1941, that instead of fracturing his vertebrae, the noose only strangled him, and the executioner had to accelerate his death by standing on his shoulders.

During preparations for an Italian religious festival in 2004, a two-metre-high metal crucifix toppled from the top of a structure and killed elderly Maddalena Camillo who happened to be walking past.

Vestal virgins in Rome who violated their vows of chastity were not crucified but buried alive.

Arthur H. Day conspired with his sister-in-law to dispose of his wife Desire, which he did on a trip to Niagara Falls by pushing into the rapids. 'Accidental death' might well have been the verdict had not the police found the tickets for their journeys – two returns and one single.

Two hundred and eighty Jews were hanged in England in 1279, having been found guilty of high treason, namely, coin-clipping –

scraping particles from coins of the realm, melting them down and manufacturing 'new' currency.

In the reign of Edward I (1272–1307), because a murderer had escaped from Exeter, not only the porter of the City's gate was hanged but the Mayor as well.

David, the last native Prince of Wales, was hanged in 1283 at Shrewsbury.

The assassins who murdered the Scottish King James I in Perth in 1437 were paraded in the market place wearing red-hot iron crowns before being drawn and quartered; their internal organs were drawn out while they watched, then their bodies were hacked into four parts and put on display.

The *Annual Register* of 1788 includes a report of the execution for forgery of one Nundcomar, who was so devout a Brahmin that he refused to allow Western hands to violate his person; on the scaffold, one of his own religion tied his blindfold and positioned the noose, the hangman released the trapdoors, and others of his religion cut the body down and carried it away for burial.

The remains of the martyr John Southworth were accidentally discovered in 1927 during excavations near the site of the English College in Douay in northern France. Much revered by the faithful, he was declared a saint in 1970.

The Greek writer Lucian (AD 117–180) recorded the bizarre method by which a female Christian martyr was executed. An ass was killed, its stomach slit open and the innards removed; the victim was then forced to occupy the interior, only her head protruding, after which the skin was sewn up again. Outside the ghastly 'coffin' the vultures did their deadly work – as did 'the eventual swarm of writhing worms within'.

The five men who in 1820 conspired in a house in Cato Street, London, to murder government ministers, break into the banks for money, seize artillery pieces from the Army and take over the Mansion House and the Tower, were hanged, then beheaded. A lady who had hired a room overlooking the execution site afterwards wrote, 'My brother Cecil, who had never seen an execution, said he wished very much to see how they [the victims] would behave, but when they were tied up, he felt so nervous and in fact felt so much more than they themselves did, that he retreated to a corner of the room and hid himself so that he might not see the drop fall, an attitude which excited great contempt in the people who were in the room with him; among them was one woman, young and pretty, and very decent looking, who kept her eyes fixed on the executions all the time and, when they had hung a few seconds, exclaimed "There's two of them not quite dead yet!" '

In her *Memoirs* Lady Bessborough recounted how, when visiting Orléans in France in 1778, she witnessed '7 or 8 dead bodies broken on the wheel a few days ago, so the bodies were quite fresh' and, while in Toulouse, 'We saw 19 or 20 dead bodies hanging on a triangular gallows, accompanied by 3 or 4 others, also wheel-broken (tied on a horizontally mounted wheel, their arms and legs then shattered with a hammer before the final blow to the heart), exhibited in full view of a public thoroughfare.'

In 1381 mobs stormed the Tower of London and captured Simon Sudbury, Archbishop of Canterbury, together with Sir Robert Hale, Chancellor of the Exchequer, and other officials. All were decapitated on Tower Hill and the Archbishop's head was carried, impaled on a lance, to London Bridge, where it was displayed to passers-by. The mob also entered the royal apartments in the Tower and terrified Richard II's mother so much that she fainted. The riot ended rapidly when Wat Tyler, the leader of the mob, was killed by the Lord Mayor of London.

Seven German prisoners-of-war were hanged in Fort Leavenworth, Kansas, USA, in 1945, for hanging Dreschler, a fellow prisoner, who had admitted giving military information to the American authorities.

After struggling with the executioner, Ewen MacDonald was hanged, then cut down, and his body was sent for dissection at Surgeon's Hall. The medical staff were busy elsewhere and, when they returned, found him sitting up. It was reported that, rather than be denied the fresh specimen they were hoping to anatomise, the surgeon picked up a wooden maul and killed poor Ewen with a blow to the head.

The crowd was thoroughly entertained at Tyburn on 2 February 1785 when twenty men were hanged on the scaffold. It was reported that 'before leaving the prison the unhappy criminals kissed each other, then marched on solemnly, two and two, singing a funeral hymn.'

In the fifteenth century, ports along the south coast of England were given the privilege of dealing with law-breakers in their own individual ways. Hastings and Dover were allowed to throw condemned felons over the cliffs into the sea; Pevensey, to drop them from the bridge into the harbour at high tide; Sandwich, to bury a man or woman alive at a place called, appropriately, the 'Thiefdowns', and Fordwich, to tie the culprit 'knee bent' and drown him in the river Stour.

The notorious gang-leader Jonathan Wild was taken to be hanged at Tyburn on 24 May 1725. On the way, true to his principles, he picked the pocket of the chaplain accompanying him. Characteristic of the intemperate habits of prison clergy of the day, the item was a corkscrew, and Wild 'died with the eloquent trophy in his hand!'

Childish innocence didn't count for much in 1808, when seven-year-old Michael Hammond and his eleven-year-old sister Mary were hanged at Lynn for felony.

Until removed from the statute books in 1820, it was a crime punishable by death to poach by night with one's face blackened, to vandalise Westminster Bridge or to be found in disguise in the Royal Mint, Tower of London.

John Bellingham shot the Prime Minister, Spencer Perceval, in the lower side of the left breast on 11 May 1812. Arrested and tried, he was hanged, but it was reported that when news of the murder reached Nottingham 'a numerous crowd publicly testified its joy by shouts, huzzas, drums beating, flags flying, bells ringing, and bonfires blazing! It was not until the military had been called out, that order was restored.'

For murdering her husband, dismembering his body and dumping the parts across London in 1726, Catharine Hayes was sentenced to be burned to death. The usual practice was for the hangman to pull on the rope which secured her by the neck to the post, thereby strangling her before the flames rose, but in trying to do so he burned his hand and retreated, leaving her to be roasted alive.

In the USA, the use of hanging ropes made from Manila hemp was customary until 1944, when the Washington authorities decreed that henceforth they should be made, instead, of agave, an American plant having tall flower stalks and fleshy leaves.

There are no reports of any condemned men insisting that tradition should be observed.

Earl Ferrers was hanged on 5 May 1760 for shooting one of his servants dead. His hat, together with the hangman's rope, was buried with him.

Iranian Khadijeh Jahed was found guilty in 2004 of murdering her lover's wife Laleh Saharkhizan, and, if the sentence is confirmed, she will be hanged; however, because she was also convicted of taking drugs, she will be flogged prior to being noosed.

The Mexican Emperor Montezuma (1390–1464) had the hearts of living victims torn out as offerings to the sun gods.

In 1603, 33,347 inhabitants of London died of the plague.

Before being escorted to the Newgate scaffold on 28 March 1805, where he was to be hanged, the convicted criminal Richard Hayward partook of bread and cheese and drank some coffee; then to his fellow convicts watching through the bars of their cells he shouted, 'Farewell, my lads, I am just a-going off; God bless you!' When they replied, 'We are sorry for you', he retorted, 'I want none of your pity, keep your snivelling till it be your own turn!'

When the French Revolutionary leader Georges-Jacques Danton mounted the scaffold to be guillotined, he surveyed the vast crowd contemptuously and said, 'Do not forget to show my head to the mob – they have not often seen one like it!'

The sentence of death passed on those guilty of high treason in seventeenth-century Scottish courts was drastic in the extreme:

'That you be taken to the Mercat Cross of Edinburgh and there to be hanged on the gibbet until you be dead, and then your head, legs, arms and remaining parts of your body to be quartered and put in public places, and your whole lands, heritages, annual rents, tax, homestead, rooms, possessions, corn, cattle, goods, gear, and sums of money pertaining to them, to be defaulted and handed over to our sovereign lord's use.'

In the Bible, the Second Book of Samuel records how Rechab and Baanah were hanged by David 'over the pool' after having their hands and feet cut off; hanged too were the two sons of Rizpah and the five sons of Michel, the daughter of Saul.

Until 1823 the cadavers of those who had committed suicide were not allowed to be interred in consecrated ground; instead they were buried at crossroads with stakes driven through their hearts. The last suicide whose corpse was so maltreated was buried at the intersection of King's Road and Grosvenor Place, in Chelsea, London, in that year.

Abdul al-Ghoraid would have been qualified to be included in this category. In 2004 he was sentenced to death for murder and was kneeling, awaiting the death-blow from the executioner's raised sword, when his victim's father, standing among the spectators, shouted his forgiveness; this, according to Islamic sharia law, granted a reprieve, and Abdul went free, no doubt greatly relieved.

It was reported in *The Death Warrant* magazine of 20 January 1844 that 'George Higinbotham, an undertaker, was employed to remove in a shell [a temporary container] the body of a woman who had died of the typhus fever. In conveying the body from the shell into the coffin, he observed that his left hand was smeared with a moisture which had oozed from it. He had a recent scratch on his thumb, and on the following morning this scratch was inflamed. In the evening he was attacked with a cold shivering and pain in his head and limbs, followed by symptoms of a severe fever and swelling. On the seventh day, delirium, extreme prostration, and coma supervened, and death took place on the tenth day.'

When Kim Jong, ruler of North Korea, discovered that a conspiracy had been hatched by some of his generals to assassinate him, he had them arrested and taken under escort to the vast May Day Stadium in the capital Pyongyang; there, before a capacity crowd, petrol was poured over the conspirators and set alight.

One stone step about halfway down the spiral stairway of the Tower of London's Bloody Tower is twice as steep as the others. In mediaeval times, anyone fleeing down the steps would not be able to avoid falling head first the rest of the way, ricocheting off the stone walls.

William Duell was sentenced to death for murder and on 24 November 1740 was duly hanged. What happened next was reported in the *Gentleman's Magazine*: 'His body was brought to Surgeons' Hall to be anatomized (dissected), but after it was stripped and laid on the operating table, and one of the servants was washing him ready to be cut open, he perceiv'd Life in him and found his Breath to come quicker and quicker; on which a Surgeon took some Ounces of Blood from him; in two Hours he was able to sit up in a chair, where he groaned very much and seemed in great agitation, but could not speak. He was then conveyed back to Newgate Prison, and the next day he ate his victuals heartily and asked for his mother. A large number of people came to marvel at the man who had cheated the hangman.' The courts evidently agreed, for instead of being re-hanged in accordance with his sentence, he was transported to the colonies for life.

The dictionary defines insufflation as 'breathing or blowing into something'. When the Curé of Peifane broke his sacred vows and aroused sexual desire in the Dame de Lieu by breathing warmly on her erogenous zones, then seducing her, he was burned at the stake; as was another French priest, Louis Gaufridi, for committing the same crime in 1611.

An Aboriginal way of killing an opponent was to sing the 'song of the dream-snake' with him in mind. This would result in the 'dream-snake' wrapping its coils about the victim whilst he was asleep and squeezing him slowly to death.

In the nineteenth century Fijians lived in houses supported on thick tree trunks, and tradition has it that, in order to prevent these supports from collapsing from damp and termites, magical protection was sought by burying a man alive at the bottom of each hole before the trunks were lowered in place.

William Ure, in his book *History of Rutherglen and East Kilbride*, published in 1874, described how 'Lindsay of Dunrode, in 1693, visited his miserable tenants, escorted by twelve soldiers mounted on white horses. While skating on the ice he had a hole made in it, and had one of his serfs, who had inadvertently disobliged him in some trifling circumstance, immediately drowned.'

In earlier centuries, men found guilty of high treason, for plotting against the monarch, were hanged, drawn and quartered on the scaffold, but not so women guilty of the same crime. The judge Sir William Blackstone (1723–1780) stated the reason: 'In treasons of every kind, the punishment of women is the same (death), and different from the men (in method). For because the decency due to the sex forbids the exposing and publicly mangling of their bodies, the sentence is, they shall be drawn to the gallows and there to be burned alive.' However in 1790 the law was altered and women were hanged instead.

Lord Stourton, hanged for murder in the sixteenth century, had earlier claimed the privilege as a peer of being suspended by a silken rope. He was, and the rope was hung over his tomb in Sarum Cathedral.

An ordinary hanging usually attracted a large crowd, but one with a woman victim always drew a vast multitude of spectators. Charles Dickens, on attending that of the murderess Maria Manning on 13 November 1849, afterwards wrote in *The Times*: 'When I joined the crowds at midnight, the shrillness and howls that were raised from time to time, denoting that they came from a concourse of boys and girls already assembled in the best places, made my blood run cold. When the day dawned, thieves, low prostitutes, ruffians and vagabonds of every kind, flocked to the ground, with every variety of offensive and foul behaviour. Fighting, faintings, whistling, brutal jokes, tumultuous demonstrations of indecent delight when swooning women with their dress disordered were dragged out of the crowd by the officers, gave a new zest to the general entertainment. When the miserable creature who had attracted all this ghastly sight about her was finally turned off and left quivering in the air, no more restraint in any of the previous obscenities was shown, and there was no belief among the crowd but that she perished as do beasts.'

DEAD-EASY RECIPES

The World Record Lobster Eating Championship of 2004 was won by Sonya Thomas of Virginia, USA, who devoured 38 lobsters, total weight 9lb 12oz, in 12 minutes.

An Eskimo, one of a group marooned on an ice-floe, not only kept himself alive by eating his companions' flesh after they had died, but escaped by constructing a kayak using their bones, and covering the frame with their tightly stretched skins.

Francis Trevelyan Buckland, an eccentric Victorian who at one time was assistant surgeon to the 2nd Life Guards, was an obsessive collector of the rare and unusual. Among his collection was a hair from the head of Henry IV (1399–1413); whether this had been removed from the royal tomb or was passed down through the ages from a fifteenth-century court barber is not known. Other items included fragments of a Siberian dinosaur. Being an ardent naturalist, he believed that most creatures, even insects, were edible, and demonstrated it by eating such unappetising dishes as flies, slugs and even broiled elephant's trunk. But perhaps his Epicurean *pièce de résistance* was that while dining with an acquaintance he is reported to have announced that, although he had had many a strange repast in his time, never before had he eaten part of a king; he then proceeded to consume the heart of Louis XIV, which, doubtless cooked, lay on his plate. If true, the desecration could probably have taken place when many of the royal tombs were vandalised during the French Revolution.

When Colonel Vajour was condemned to death by the French Revolutionaries, he asked at what time he would be executed. When told that it would be at two o'clock, he replied, 'That is a pity, it is my usual dinner-hour; but never mind, I'll dine a little earlier!'

In 1994 an American woman buttered a slice of bread, placed cheese on it, then toasted the repast. The cheese bubbled and shrivelled and an image of a female face appeared, which the woman identified as that of the Virgin Mary. She kept it for ten years, then advertised it on the internet. An offer of £15,000 was accepted.

In recent centuries 'Ale Conners' were annually elected to test the strength of the beer produced in the City of London. This they did by pouring a pool of the beverage over a bench, then sitting in it; if they stuck to the seat, the quality was pronounced satisfactory. There must surely have been better ways . . .

King John lusted after Maud the Fair, daughter of Baron Fitzwalter. She rejected his advances and her father objected so much that the King exiled him to France. To further his intentions, the King then had Maud imprisoned in the round turret of the White Tower in the Tower of London. When she still scorned him, he sent her a poisoned egg in her food; she ate it and died. Later her father returned to England and joined other barons in their endeavours to bring the King to heel, efforts which resulted in John agreeing to make his mark on the Magna Carta. So it could be said that the document which gave us all our freedom started with a poisoned egg in the round turret of the White Tower.

In January 1930 Selina Gilmore entered a restaurant in Alabama and ordered some sandwiches and eggs. The sandwiches were brought but, during the delay while the eggs were being prepared, she started to cause a disturbance and was asked to leave the premises; she did, only to return with a shotgun, with which she shot dead the man behind the counter. She met her death in the electric chair.

American Emilene Meeker murdered her niece and was executed in March 1883. Her last breakfast consisted of a large beefsteak, three potatoes, a piece of meat pie, bread and butter, and coffee. For lunch she managed two boiled eggs, one potato, two slices of toast, a doughnut and, of course, more coffee. Obviously she had no worries about having indigestion later.

When the Lord Mayor of London invited George III to an official banquet in the Guildhall in November 1761, the cost totalled £6,898 5s 4d (£1 in that century was equivalent to £100 today). A completely new dinner service, consisting of thousands of pieces of crockery, was purchased, on which to eat, among other delicacies, ducks' tongues. Six 'necessary women' were also employed – one assumes as servers.

Before being executed, American murderer Charles Singleton's last meal consisted of fried eggplant, potato salad, barbecued baked beans, green tomatoes, double-cheese soybean patties and sweet potatoes, followed by two vanilla doughnuts, washed down with two Cokes. Hardly a meal to die for.

Fears of a terrorist attack closed a Brussels underground station in February 2004 when white powder, suspected of being highly toxic, was found scattered in a phone booth; the station was reopened when the powder was found to be fine sugar, spilled by some clumsy croissant-eater.

Much favoured locally in the City of Bath, 'bath chaps' are the cheeks of pigs, sold as conical delicacies.

In the early spring of 1790 women were attacked by a man who was quickly given the name of 'The Monster' by the newspapers. Night patrols were organised, and a reward of £70 offered for his capture. He was eventually caught and sentenced to seven years' transportation, but while awaiting the prison ship he held lavish banquets in Newgate Gaol. The *Oracle* of 20 August of that year reported how 'the Monster sent cards to about twenty couples, among whom were some of his alibi friends, his brothers, sisters, and several of the prisoners. At four o'clock the party sat to tea; this being over, two violins struck up, accompanied by a flute, and the company proceeded to exercise their limbs. The merry dancing continued till eight o'clock, when the company took a cold supper and a variety of wines, such as would not disgrace the most sumptuous gala, and about nine o'clock departed, that being the usual time for locking the doors of the prison.' His sentence was later reduced to six years in gaol.

When Scottish farmworker Robert Smith was given a life sentence for culpable homicide in 1893, his employer visited him and said that a petition was being raised to obtain a reprieve; at that Smith was alleged to have exclaimed, 'Dae no such thing – I was never so happy in my life! The meat is gude and aye sure, and ye hae a roof abune your heid. It's far better than howing neeps (hoeing turnips) or howkin' tatties (lifting potatoes)!'

Citizens of Far East countries find that powdered deer antlers boost their virility.

The Romanian Prince Vlad the Impaler (1431–1476) not only ate the flesh of his enemies but, rather than waste the blood, spread it on bread and ate it.

In the early 1800s the Indian Gaikwar of Baroda disposed of awkward citizens by administering them food impregnated with diamond dust.

The Greek physician Galen (b. AD 131) believed that to be healthy, the body had to maintain a balance between being hot and cold: a disease with chills was treated with heating drugs; one with fever, with cooling drugs. So drugs containing bitter almonds were administered to those with a chill, and drugs containing cucumber seeds were given to those with a fever – hence the widely used expression 'as cool as a cucumber'.

The last meal ordered by American serial killer John Wayne Gacy before being executed was fried chicken, french fries, fried shrimp and strawberries.

Innkeeper Benjamin Wilson was remanded for the Grand Jury, the charge being that, at 7 a.m. on 15 July 1620, several men, including Richard Durrell, the constable, 'were found so drunk that they were lying in their own vomit like swine, and on Holy Thursday, Robert Fylde drank so much that he was unable to speak to the vicar'.

The *Glasgow Medical Journal* in 1859 reported the case of a baker's daughter who was able to remain in her father's oven for twelve minutes, apparently unaffected by its temperature of 274 degrees.

In 2004 taste experts claimed that the finest coffee in the world is Kopi Luwak, made from beans which have first been passed through the intestines of civets (Indonesian cats), a process which, it is claimed, removes the drink's bitter taste and replaces it with a more acceptable flavour. Such a delicacy has to be paid for, of course, although at £230 per pound there might well be grounds for complaint.

Before being taken to be beheaded, on 21 January 1793, Queen Marie Antoinette was given a cup of chocolate and a bread roll by the gaoler's wife.

A medical papyrus of 1560 BC, discovered in 1872, contains prescriptions including such ingredients as beer – not ordinary beer but different varieties such as Sweet Beer Froth of Beer, and Swill-of-Beer. Water had to be Water-from-the-Bird-Pond or even Water-in-which-the-Phallus-had-been-Washed. To cure the 'Great Debility', the papyrus prescribed taking Excrement-of-the-Adu-Bird cooked in Sweet Beer, and to 'Dye one's Hair', mix Tapeworm, Hoof of an Ass and Vulva of a Bitch.

Most German spies landing in this country during World War II brought with them a wireless transmitting set, a code book, some English currency – and a large portion of German sausage.

So gluttonous was Edward IV that immediately after a feast he would make himself vomit in order to start on another bout of gorging.

In mediaeval times, the cure for those suffering from the ague, a malarial fever inducing uncontrollable shivering, was to swallow a spider wrapped in its cobweb. The recipe did not stipulate whether the best results depended on swallowing the spider while it was still alive or not.

Until advances in modern medicine, no tests existed which would enable a doctor carrying out a postmortem to identify whether the victim of a suspected murder had been poisoned. One primitive method, having opened the stomach, was to taste the liquids remaining therein; if bitter, murder most foul had been committed.

When Napoleon was a prisoner on St Helena he was ill with either an ulcer or cancer, and his doctor gave him tartar emetic in a glass of lemonade. This made Napoleon even more ill. Next time he had the pains, the doctor repeated the medicine, but Napoleon passed it secretly to his attendant Montholan, who then also became violently ill – so, for the remaining few months of his life, Napoleon dispensed entirely with the services of his physician.

Consumption was a much feared ailment in the 1700s, but perhaps preferable to one cure which consisted of snails boiled in milk, or another involving live woodlice boiled in ale.

In the days when people took their dough to the bakery to be made into loaves, eight bakers and two 'bakeresses' were, in 1327, tried for fraud. The indictment of one of them stated 'that when his neighbours and others came with their dough for the kneading thereof, the said John used to put the dough over a hole in the table, and had one of his household sitting in secret beneath it and, carefully opening it, the servant withdrew some of the dough, frequently collecting great quantities, to the great loss to the neighbours.' The guilty ones were punished by having to stand in the pillory with some of the dough hung round their necks, and the two bakeresses were committed to Newgate Gaol.

In the early nineteenth century, physician Samuel Hahnemann believed that certain diseases could be treated with homeopathic drugs derived from plants which resembled the part of the body which was diseased. The nutmeg vaguely resembles the brain, so could be used in treating brain diseases; the black spot in the flower euphrasia – eyebright – resembles the pupil of the eye, so should be applied to diseases of the eye; and disease of the testicle could be cured by using the root of the orchid, because not only does its shape resemble that of the testicle, but the word *orchid* itself, from the Greek *orchis*, means 'testicle'.

For his last meal, Canadian Leo Anthony Mantha, scheduled to be executed on 27 April 1959, ordered a T-bone steak; the meat had to be cut into small pieces, and the only utensil permitted was a spoon. Shortly afterwards he was hanged in a disused lift shaft converted into a gallows.

John Fisher, Bishop of Rochester, was held in the Tower of London under sentence of death for refusing to acknowledge the royal supremacy as demanded by Henry VIII. One day he was left without food and, when he asked his gaoler about it, the man replied that he had heard that the prisoner was to be executed that day and so the food would be wasted. To which the Bishop retorted, 'Thou seest me still alive, and therfore whatsoeuer newes thou shalt heare of me hereafter, let me no more lacke my dinner, but make yt readie as thou art wont to doe, and yf thou seest me dead when thou commest, then eat it thyself; but I promise thee, yf I be alive, I mind by god's grace, to eate neuer a bitt the lesse!'

Theodore Durrant murdered two young women in 1898 and hid their bodies in a church steeple in San Francisco. Scores of reporters packed around the gallows in San Quentin Prison, among them the condemned man's father and mother. After being hanged, the body was taken into the next room. The parents apparently, and understandably, seemed upset at seeing their son's cadaver but, when asked whether they'd like a cup of tea, said they'd prefer a full meal. Accordingly a table was set, a few feet from the coffin, and the couple sat down and started the meal. A newsman later reported to his editor that he'd heard Mrs Durrant say brightly, 'Papa, do give me some more of the roast!'

Because a guest at a wedding in the Philippines in 2004 happened to touch the bride's posterior, other guests attacked and killed him, then roasted some of his body parts and served them at the celebratory party.

Squid and octopus make good eating, but not the latter when it's of the blue-ringed variety, as some Vietnam villagers found out after eating some in 2004, for two people died of its poison and 85 others were rushed to hospital for medical treatment.

It was reported in a Paris newspaper in 1985 that the only surviving bottle of Chateau Lafitte 1787 had been bought by the wealthy Forbes family for the sum of $157,500; but the purchase left a bitter taste in the new owner's mouth when it was found that the cork had slowly slipped down into the bottle and ruined the precious contents.

An eighteenth-century recipe to keep an old man fit and well prescribed 'a little wine; avoid carrots, but parsnips are nourishing, and the passions demand great regard, so it is not worth his while to get angry.'

During Elizabeth I's reign a law was passed forbidding the eating of flesh on the prescribed Fish Days or at any time during Lent; offenders would be fined £3 or three months in prison; any person aware of anyone breaking that law, who did not immediately report it to the authorities, would be fined 40 shillings.

The blowfish, considered a rare delicacy in Japan, is nevertheless the most poisonous fish in the world, giving the diner but minutes to live, and only highly skilled chefs are licensed to prepare it. Should one of the chefs fail to remove all the toxic organs before serving the dish, and thereby bring about the death of the customer, he is honour-bound to commit harakiri: disembowel himself in the same horrific manner as did the Samurai warriors of old.

A lion having attacked an African village in 2004 and killed a woman, her husband, instead of burying her, laced her mutilated corpse with poison and left it where the animal would find it. He got his revenge when, on going to the spot later, he found what was left of his spouse – and one very dead lion.

When the French Cardinal Richelieu was at the point of death, a female quack-doctor administered a mixture of horse dung in white wine. He died.

Early Egyptian doctors administered medicine to their patients, some of the prescriptions consisting of opium, squill and even human excrement. The urine of a faithful wife was considered to be particularly effective in healing sore eyes.

For a pub bet two Australian men chewed the tails off live mice; one even attempted to eat the rodent as well, but then spat it out. The local RSPCA officials were not amused; nor, no doubt, were the mice.

In 1848 murderer James Rush was allowed to have his meals in a local hotel while awaiting trial, and on one occasion sent a note to the chef: 'Pig today, and plenty of plum sauce!'

In South Korea in 2004 three hungry men killed their employer's dog and used it as the main ingredient of their traditional dish of dog meat soup, which they proceeded to consume; their boss is now suing them for the loss of his pet.

Princess Elizabeth was imprisoned in the Tower by Queen Mary, who suspected that her half-sister might be implicated in a plot to overthrow her. When, on 19 May 1554, Elizabeth was released, she celebrated her freedom by having a dinner of pork and beans at the nearby King's Head in Fenchurch Street.

The Christian martyr Saint Laurence was sentenced to death by the Romans in AD 258. He was secured to a gridiron, a framework of thin iron bars, and a fire was started underneath. As the cruelly slow grilling took effect, he, with defiant humour, called to the executioner, 'This side is roasted enough, oh tyrant great; decide whether roasted or raw thou thinkest the better meat!'

Charles IX always carried a popular cure-all, a bezoar stone, the gall-stone of an animal, with him, believing that it would prevent him from being poisoned. But his royal surgeon, Ambroise Paré, denied it had any magical qualities. On learning that a criminal was about to be executed by being strangled in public, he offered the man the alternative of taking poison and then swallowing the stone. The felon jumped at the chance of escaping the executioner and took some poison, then the bezoar. After seven hours in convulsions, he died an agonising death. But you can't convince some people, for the King then swore that the stone was just a pebble, not a genuine bezoar.

In 2004 Thai drug addict Phosaeng killed his eight-year-old brother, cut out his heart and liver, added salt, chilli and rice – and ate them.

A traffic jam in the full meaning of the word was caused when, in February 2004, a tanker full of raspberry syrup, en route to a jam factory in Bavaria, sprang a leak and left a 25-mile trail of the sticky liquid along a German autobahn.

To cure epilepsy, the treatment prescribed by the fourteenth-century surgeon John of Gaddesden was a mixture of boar's bladder and mistletoe, stirred up with 'extract of cuckoo', because he believed that the bird had epilepsy itself once a month.

KINGLY DEEDS AND MISDEEDS

Anne Boleyn's brother George, found guilty of incest and adultery with his sister, was beheaded on the orders of Henry VIII on 17 May 1536.

The sculptor Bernini had to make a bust from a portrait of Charles I, but found the task difficult, saying that 'there was something so unfortunate about the facial features, that the subject was bound to meet a violent end.' When finished, the bust was sent to England and displayed in a garden to the King. As he and the courtiers were viewing it, a hawk flew overhead, a partridge in its claws, and some of its blood fell on the neck of the bust. The occurrence was viewed as a prediction of the King's death; he was beheaded in public in 1649.

During the reign of Edward I (1272–1307) it was decreed that one inch would be defined as the length of three dry, round grains of barley touching each other.

Until the late 1600s men played the female roles on the stage. On one occasion, when Charles II expressed impatience at the delay in the curtain going up, the stage manager said, 'Sire, the scene will commence as soon as the queen has shaved!'

When funerals occurred in George III's time, gentlemen were expected to carry black swords, and muffle the sound of their shoes with pieces of chamois.

The Prince of Wales, who later became George V, served as a naval cadet in HMS *Constant* in the Pacific. On 11 June 1881 he entered the following in the ship's log. 'At 4 a.m. the *Flying Dutchman* crossed our bows. She emitted a strange phosphorescent light as of a phantom ship all aglow, in the midst of which light the mast, spars and sails of a brig 200 yards distant stood out in strong relief as she came up on the port bow, where the officer of the watch from the bridge saw her, as did also the quarter-deck midshipman, who was sent forward at once to the forecastle, but on arriving, there was no vestige nor any sign whatsoever of any material ship to be seen either near or right away to the horizon, the night being clear and the sea calm.'

The significance of the saying 'The King is dead, long live the King' is that the sovereignty continues automatically, the next in line immediately taking over the role; an ancient tradition, now discontinued, decreed that when a monarch was dying, the crown had to be placed nearby, so that the Prince of Wales could symbolically pick it up at the crucial moment.

The last occasion on which the King's Champion appeared at a coronation, with the duty of challenging anyone who doubted the new sovereign's right to the throne, was at the coronation of George III on 22 September 1761. It was reported that 'when he did, a white glove fell from one of the spectators in the balcony, and on it being handed to the Champion, he demanded who was his opponent? The glove was said to have been thrown by a young chevalier, who was present in female attire!'

Kingston-upon-Thames in Surrey is so called because of the preservation there of the King's Stone, upon which seven Saxon kings are said to have been enthroned. It was last used for that purpose in 998, after which William the Conqueror decided that Westminster Abbey would be more appropriate.

At a major fire in St James' Street in April 1733, George II and the Prince of Wales, who were present, were so impressed by the efforts of the firemen 'that His Majesty ordered twenty guineas to be shared among the firemen, and not to be outdone, the Prince gave them ten guineas'.

When the Duke of Atholl was sentenced to death in November 1306, Edward I ordered that because the Duke had always claimed to be of royal descent, he should be hanged on gallows 50 feet high. And so he was.

Henry VIII tried to jump a ditch in 1525, fell into deep mud and had to be helped out by a footman: had he not been, history might have been very different.

When Edward II was crowned on 24 February 1307, as reported by the historian Holinshed, 'There was such a press and throng at this coronation that a knight, Sir John Bakewell, was thrown off his horse and crushed to death.'

The *Annals* record the hideous end suffered by Edward II: 'In the year of Our Lord 1327, the 21 September, by treason of Roger Mortimer, Edward II, King of England, was slain while sleeping in Corfe Castle [actually Berkeley Castle in Gloucestershire]; for, taking a certain great table, they placed it on his body, pressing down the four corners, and seizing on a spit with the point red-hot, they thrust it into him *in secretioribus*. And so he was slain and buried at Gloucester.'

George V died in 1936, but it was not until 1968 that it was disclosed that his doctor had accelerated his death with a lethal injection.

The embalming of the body of William the Conqueror went sadly awry, with the result that not only did the corpse swell and split the coffin open, but the nauseating smell of decomposing flesh caused the funeral service to be hastily concluded.

In 1770 Lord Grosvenor sued the Duke of Cumberland for damages of £100,000 for seducing his wife, while at the same time the Duke of Grafton was divorcing his spouse for adultery. The King, when opening Parliament, drily observed that 'distemper among the horned cattle has lately broken out!'

The Monument, on Fish Street Hill, was originally intended by Sir Christopher Wren to be just a hollow shaft, to be used for astronomical purposes, with a statue of Charles II on the top.

In Volume XXVI of *Archaeologia*, 1832, can be found the description of the remains of Henry IV (d. 1413): 'When the coffin was opened in that year, the skin being the thickness of leather, the beard thick and matted, the teeth perfect except for one missing fore-tooth. The eyes were still in their sockets, the flesh on the nose moist and clammy.'

In later life Henry VIII became so overweight that he could move about only with the aid of a crane-like apparatus.

Walter Tyrrel, a marksman of some distinction, nevertheless loosed an arrow which ricocheted off the trunk of a tree and killed William II on 2 August 1100. Wisely he paused not on his departure; riding to the coast, he promptly embarked for France, where as a penance he joined the Crusades.

Displayed in the mausoleum built in Inner Mongolia to preserve the sacred image of the Mongol conqueror Genghis Khan (1162–1227) is his ceremonial butter-dish, which is kept ever burning. Each year the conqueror's wooden bucket is filled to the brim with mare's milk, in accordance with the traditional belief that the direction in which the milk leaks out of the vessel is that from which prosperity will come to the Mongol people.

At the coronation of young Edward VI in 1547, an acrobat entertained the royals and the crowds by performing balancing tricks on a rope stretched outside St Paul's Cathedral.

John Harvey, appointed by James I to be his personal physician, took full advantage of the post by making outrageous remarks, such as describing a prolonged belch 'as being comparable to a motion from the House of Commons to the House of Lords!'

William III (1689–1702) continually worried about his health, even writing to foreign doctors under an assumed name to get unprejudiced opinions of his symptoms – opinions which were always unfavourable. He suffered from malaria and a racking cough and also had boils, which he dusted with a mixture of flour and the dry, powdered eyes of crabs. None of these afflictions actually killed him – his death was hastened when he fell off his horse and suffered a fracture of his right collar bone.

James I certainly used his royal prerogative to the full. Following his coronation he created two earls, ten barons and 62 Knights of the Bath, and conferred the honour of knighthood on no fewer than four hundred gentlemen.

An eye-witness, describing the scene following the guillotining of Louis XVI, wrote how 'A number of armed volunteers crowded to dip in the blood of the despot their pikes, their bayonets, their sabres. Several officers of the Marseillaise battalion and others dipped the covers of letters in this impure blood, and carried them on the points of their swords at the head of their companies, exclaiming "This is the blood of a tyrant!" One citizen got up on the scaffold and plunged his whole arm into the blood of

Louis, of which a great deal remained; he took handfuls of the clotted gore and sprinkled it over the crowd pressing around the scaffold, each anxious to receive a drop on his forehead. "Friends," exclaimed this citizen, "We were threatened that the blood of Louis should be on our heads – and so you see it is!" '

If there's anything wrong with the rooms, complain to the management! That's exactly what Henry III (1216–1272) did regarding the garderobe (lavatory) in the royal apartments in the Tower of London. Writing to the Constable of the Tower, he said angrily, 'Since the privy chamber of our Wardrobe Tower is situated in an undue and improper place, wherefore it smells badly, we command that you cause another privy to be made, even though it should [might] cost a hundred pounds.' He could have added 'Or heads will roll!' but probably didn't need to.

Although those of the Tudor dynasty chose green and white as their favourite colours, wearing anything green was earlier considered to be a sign of moral turpitude or depravity, adopted by those of easy or non-existent morals.

William IV (d. 1837) occasionally put on his 'plainer' clothes and strolled around the streets alone. One day, in Pall Mall, he met a court acquaintance, Watson-Taylor, took his arm and wandered along St James' Street, where he was soon followed by a noisy mob; a woman came up and kissed him. Two other friends witnessed the scene and, as the crowd became menacing, the trio managed to get His Majesty back to the Palace, although one of his escort was shoved and kicked about en route. When the dangers were diplomatically pointed out to him, the King exclaimed genially, 'Oh, never mind all that; when I've walked about a few times they will get used to it, and will take no notice!'

Henry II (1154–1189) was crowned with a German crown brought to England by his mother Matilda, Emperor Henry V's widow.

Before setting sail for Palestine, bound for the Crusades, Richard I (1189–1199) warned the crew that any seaman killing another on board ship would be tied to the corpse and thrown into the sea.

James I (1603–1625) referred to smoking as 'a custom loathsome to the eye, hateful to the nose, harmful to the brain, dangerous to the lungs, and in the black, stinking fume thereof, nearly resembling the horrible Stygian smoke of the pit that is bottomless'.

Every mace borne by mace-bearers is being carried upside down – even the one in the House of Commons. Originally they were clubs used to defend the Sovereign or their representative, the Lord Mayor or Mayor, but they became more ornamental, being engraved with the Royal Arms and/or the insignia of the city or town. The flanged head – the 'hitting' end – was no longer needed in its offensive role and decreased in size until it was smaller than the boss that bore the ornamentation. By the end of the fifteenth century it had become no longer logical or convenient to hold the mace with its head uppermost, so the Mace-Bearers or Sergeants-at-Mace inverted the erstwhile weapon and carried it with the now heavier, decorated end at the top and the original 'warhead' at the bottom.

Charles I owned a ring which could be used as both a sundial and a calculator.

George I was crowned on 20 October 1714. He did not understand English, and few of those present at the coronation could speak German, so they had to explain the ceremonies to him in as much Latin as they knew. This gave rise to the popular jest 'that much bad language had passed between the King and his ministers that day!'

The Prince of Wales, later George IV (1820–1830) and the Duke of York were once stopped in their carriage on Hay Hill, Berkeley Square, and robbed by highwaymen. With them were Colonel Lowther and General Hulse. All were returning from a house of ill-repute in Berkeley Street and, when money was demanded, all they could muster between them was half-a-crown. Must have been a very expensive group of ladies!

During the coronation of Stephen in 1135 a violent storm arose 'which threw all parties into such confusion that the consecrated wafer fell to the ground, the kiss of peace after the sacrament was omitted, and even the final benediction forgotten'.

The version of *The Hangman's Record* published in 1926 records that 'in the rear of Whitehall is a statue of James II, the finger of whose hand points to the spot where his sire [Charles I] was decapitated. The obscure pedestal, which represents a monarch who abdicated his throne, is said to portray grief in a manner never excelled by any other sculpture.'

The original Tudor coat of arms was a red shield with a chevron separating three bleeding Saxon heads.

Following the death of Edward IV in 1483 his corpse, naked but for a loincloth, was displayed to crowds of his grieving subjects for twelve hours, then lay in state in St Stephen's Chapel, Westminster.

On 24 May 1618 James I decreed that the populace might, following Sunday church services, take part in 'Dancing (men and women), Archery for men, Leaping, Vaulting, May Games and Morris Dancing' but 'at all times, in the meaner sort of people, Bowling is prohibited by Law.'

Although not a royal, Oliver Cromwell insisted on decidedly regal trappings when arranging his lying-in-state. One feature was a magnificent effigy 'as made as in life, in wax, and apparelled in velvet, gold-lace and ermine'. It was laid upon the bed of state and carried on the hearse in the funeral procession. Both were deposited in Westminster Abbey, but at the time of the Restoration of Charles II to the throne the hearse was broken into pieces, and the effigy hung by the neck from a window in Whitehall before being destroyed.

The Anglo-Saxon King Aethlred was repeatedly flogged by his mother with candles, so severely that he became insensible with pain and dreaded candles for the rest of his life.

Royalty of old frequently travelled around the country accompanied by a vast retinue and stayed in stately homes; the demand for hospitality became overwhelming. Protests dared not be raised, of course, but one method of complaint was devised in 1604 when James I was hunting at Royston and happened to notice that Jowler, one of his favourite hounds, was missing. The dog eventually turned up with a note tied to its collar, which bore the message: 'Good Mr Jowler, we pray you speak to the King – for he hears you every day so doth he not us – that it will please His Majesty to go back to London, or else the country will be undone; all our provisions are already spent, and we are not able to entertain him any longer!'

The Treason Act of 1351 defined the activities that the state classed as treasonable: 'when a man doth compass (carry out) or imagine (plan) the death of our lord the king or of our lady the queen, or if a man do violate the king's companion or the king's eldest daughter unmarried, or the wife of the king's eldest son and heir, or if a man do levy war against our lord the king in his realm, or be adherent to the king's enemies in this realm, giving to them aid and comfort in the realm or elsewhere.' The violation of women of the royal family would be treason because any children thus born would alter the royal succession.

Restrictions on the use of leather during Henry VIII's reign included such clauses as 'No shoemaker shall make any boots, shoes, buskins, startups or pantoffles unless they use Leather well and truly tanned' and 'No Tanner shall tan any Hides, Calves' skin or Sheeps' skin, with hot or warm woozes. Any such offence carries the penalty of £10 and to stand in the pillory on three market days.' So if you're wearing your pantoffles, don't wooze them!

James I was incapable of walking until the age of six – reportedly because he had been fed 'the bad milk of a drunken wet-nurse' – and later in life his teeth were severely decayed, causing him to bolt his food, which frequently brought about colic and indigestion.

In 1649 Charles I, sentenced to death by the axe, knelt over the execution block and gave the executioner the signal to strike by spreading his arms wide. The gloves he wore while doing so are displayed in the Lambeth Palace Library, London.

Robert the Bruce, King of Scotland, told his friend Sir James Douglas that on his death, because he had not fulfilled his vow to assist in the Crusades, his heart should be buried in the Holy Land. Accordingly it was removed from his corpse and placed in a silver case, which Sir James wore, suspended round his neck, when he set out on the journey. While passing through Spain he joined the Spaniards in their fight against the Moors but, being overwhelmed by the enemy, tore the case from his neck and threw it in front of him, shouting 'Pass on as thou were wont – I will follow or die!' He was killed and the heart, found under his body, was brought back to Scotland by Sir Simon Locard and interred behind the High Altar of Melrose Abbey.

So thick was the ice covering the River Thames in the harsh winter of 1537 that Henry VIII, his consort Jane Seymour and a multitude of courtiers, men-at-arms, servants and lackeys rode along it on horseback to the royal palace at Greenwich.

Throughout his life James I had a marked aversion to swords, attributed to the fact that his mother, Mary, Queen of Scots, while pregnant with him, witnessed the brutal murder of her Italian secretary David Rizzio. The result of his aversion was, as described by Sir Kenelme Digby: 'When he dubbed me Knight, in the ceremony of putting the point of a naked sword on my shoulder, he could not endure to look upon it, but turned his face another way, insomuch, that in lieu of touching my shoulder, he almost thrust the point into my eyes, had not the Duke of Buckingham guided his hand aright.'

Following George IV's coronation in 1820, crowds filled Westminster Hall, cheering and applauding their new King. It was reported by one of the court ladies that he 'behaved very indecently; he was continually nodding and winking at Lady Conyngham, and sighing and making eyes at her. At one time he took a diamond brooch from his breast and, looking at her, kissed it, on which she took off her glove and kissed a ring she had on! Anybody who could have seen his disgusting figure, with a wig, the curls of which hung down his back, and quite bending beneath the weight of his robes and his sixty years would have been quite sick!'

A vault in St George's Chapel, Windsor, contains the coffins of two kings: one is Henry VIII, two of whose wives lost their heads, the other Charles I, who lost his own.

Mediaeval kings adopted a certain shade of scarlet as a royal colour, and commoners were strictly forbidden to wear it. The liveries worn by the Yeoman Warders of the Tower of London, the Yeomen of the Guard and similar royal servants are of that particular hue. The origin of the scarlet coats worn by huntsmen is that formerly no one was allowed to hunt, even on his own land, unless he had a licence to do so from the Crown, because all hunting belonged to the King. Hence hunting was allowed by pleasure of the Crown, huntsmen took part in what was a royal sport by royal permission, and for this royal sport they wore the King's livery of scarlet.

In May 1774 the tomb of Edward I, who had died in 1307, was opened and officials present reported that even after more than four and a half centuries 'they found his body, crown and velvet well perfect; the flesh of his lips and cheeks was sound and his hands well-preserved, except that one had lost its nails. There was a gauze over the face which had grown into the grain and they could not lift it up. His measure was six feet two inches.'

Some Roman emperors were buried in a sleeping position. By tradition their unfortunate servants were killed and their corpses placed in graves nearby, not lying down but kneeling, as if ready to serve their masters in the next world.

In the 1680s Charles II owed William Penn £16,000 (about £1,600,000 in today's currency), so His Majesty granted Penn the right to a vast area of the American colony which eventually took the name of Pennsylvania. In return Penn agreed to pay the King 'Two beaver skins to bee delivered att our said Castle of Windsor on the first day of January in every yeare, and also the fifth parte of all gold and silver Ore which may from time to time be found.'

Old books about the English regalia rated highly the magnificent aquamarine stone that surmounted one of the crowns, but about a hundred and fifty years ago it was discovered to be nothing more than a piece of blue glass. It is believed that the original stone was taken to France by James II in 1689 and may have been the blue stone he is said to have carried in his breeches pocket, which was never found.

Security in the court of Henry VIII was understandably tight. Anyone responsible for causing blood to be shed suffered the loss of his right hand, the amputation being carried out in accordance with a detailed procedure. 'Before the Marshall of the Court, the Sergeant of the Woodyard brought blocks and cords and bound the hand to be severed in a convenient position. The Master Cook was present with his knife, which he handed to the Sergeant of the Larder, who adjusted it and held it while the Surgeon performed the amputation. The Sergeant of the Poultry was nearby with a cock which was to have its head cut off on the block with the same knife, and the body of which was afterwards used to wrap around the wrist stump. The Yeoman of the Scullery stood close, tending a coal fire, with the Sergeant Farrier ready to hand the searing irons to the Surgeon. The Chief Surgeon seared the stump and the Groom of the Salcery held vinegar and water in case the victim fainted. The Sergeant of the Ewry and the Yeoman Chandry attended with basons and towels for the Surgeon. After the hand had been struck off, and the stump seared, the Sergeant of the Pantry offered bread, and the Sergeant of the Cellar, a pot of red wine to the sufferer.'

QUEENLY DEEDS AND MISDEEDS

Edward I's Queen Eleanor died in Derbyshire. On the journey bringing her body back to London, the King stopped overnight at least twelve times, at each place later having an 'Eleanor Cross' erected. Only three have survived, at Geddington, Waltham Cross and near Northampton. The one at Charing Cross is a replica.

Mary II (1662–1694) was married to William of Orange when she was only 15 years old.

Her Majesty Queen Elizabeth II is the 'Seigneur of the Swans', for those birds are classed as royal. Furthermore the whale is a royal mammal, and the sturgeon is classed as a royal fish.

It was once the practice for royalty to show humility to the people by washing the feet of a few. In Elizabethan times the Yeomen of the Laundry would wash people's feet, whereupon the Queen marked them with the sign of the cross and kissed them. This practice has been replaced by the sovereign awarding money on Maundy Thursday in Westminster Abbey.

A brass plate in the floor at the entrance to the Queen's private room in the Palace of Holyrood House marks the spot where David Rizzio, secretary to Mary, Queen of Scots, was brutally murdered in 1566 by a group of Scottish nobles.

In the days of Elizabeth I, members of the Company of Barber-Surgeons would display a large glass jar full of blood in their shop window as a sign that they were qualified either to give you a short back and sides or to apply a leech to the appropriate part of your body, as the case might be.

Mary I of England was also Queen of France for one year, 1560, having married the Dauphin two years earlier.

Elizabeth I's favourite colour was green.

The longest reigning English sovereign was Queen Victoria, who came to the throne on 20 June 1837 and died on 22 January 1901, a total of 63 years and seven months.

In addition to the remains of the executed Mary, Queen of Scots, the vault of Westminster Abbey also contains those of the sixteen infants of Queen Anne and the ten children of James II.

The Duchess of Buckingham had a dwarf in her retinue named Jeffrey Hudson, who was but three feet nine inches tall. At a regal entertainment given for Charles I and his consort Queen Henrietta Maria, Mr Hudson, dressed in silks and satins, was served up in a cold pie.

Remarkably Catherine de Valois was the daughter of a King (Charles VI of France), the wife of a King (Henry V), the mother of a King (Henry VI) and the grandmother of a King (Henry VII).

When an author offended Elizabeth I in a book he'd written, she had his right hand chopped off.

Nine months after Louis XVI had been guillotined in Paris during the French Revolution, his consort Queen Marie Antoinette met the same terrible fate. Her last words on the scaffold were 'Farewell, my children, I go to rejoin your father.'

In Elizabeth I's time, there were no microscopes and no second hands on watches; many people measured time by how long it took to sing particular psalms. The 'Minute Waltz' would have been really useful when boiling eggs!

Triple tragedies struck the royal household when, in 1819, Princess Charlotte's doctor left her in labour for 52 hours; not only was the child stillborn, but her mother died shortly afterwards – and the doctor shot himself.

The Imperial State Crown used at coronations contains 2,783 diamonds, 277 pearls (one of which is from the River Conway on the Welsh border), eighteen sapphires, eleven emeralds and five rubies. At its front is positioned the Second Star of Africa; it weighs just over 309 carats, and is the second largest cut diamond in existence. From the crown's arches are suspended four large pear-shaped pearls, reputed to have been the earrings of Elizabeth I.

Doubts were raised over the claim that the preserved finger found in a coffin opened in Palestine in 1982 was that of the late Grand Duchess Elisabeth, sister of Tsarina Alexandra, who was murdered in 1918.

Elizabeth I's heart is in the same small casket in Westminster Abbey as that of Mary I.

When Professor Wilhelm Conrad Roentgen discovered X-rays in 1895 Queen Amelia of Portugal arranged for X-rays to be taken of the sixteen-inch waists of her over-corseted maids-in-waiting, and pointed out the effect the constriction was having on their livers and other internal organs.

During the reign of Queen Anne (1702–1714) four 'Indian Kings', as they were called, visited England to ask for her assistance against the French in Canada. Their names were Tee Yee Neen Ho Ga Prow and Sa Ga Yean Qua Prah Ion of the Maquas Tribe; Elow Oh Kaom and Oh Nee Yeath Ion No Prow of the river Sachem, together with the Ganajoh-hore Sachem. On 18 April 1710 they went to St James' Palace for an audience with Her Majesty, where their speech was read by an interpreter, Major Pidgeon (in pidgin English?!). After making their plea for assistance, in which they stated that 'they had hung up the kettle and taken up the war-hatchet', they returned to Canada aboard HMS *Dragon* on 18 May.

The founder of the Tudor dynasty was the Welsh prince Owen Tudor, who, while dancing during a royal ball, lost his balance and fell across the knees of Queen Catherine. They became friends and, after her husband Henry V died, married. Their eldest son was the father of Henry VII, whose son was Henry VIII. Catherine died in 1437, and in the later War of the Roses Owen fought on the Lancastrian side, was captured by the Yorkists and at Hereford was sentenced to death. A chronicler described the scene: 'waving all away and trusting that he would not be beheaded, till he saw the axe and the block, and when he was in his doublet, he trusted on pardon and grace, till the collar of his red velvet doublet was ripped off. Then he said "This head shall lie on the block, that was wont to lie on Queen Catherine's lap" and put his heart and mind wholly unto God and full meekly took his death.' After the execution Tudor's head was exposed on the market cross for some time, and it was reported that 'a mad woman combed his hair and washed the blood off his face, and she got candles and set them about his face.' The corpse was buried within the Grey Friars Church, Hereford, which centuries later was demolished. Large bones discovered on the site in 1933 were believed by some to be Owen's remains.

Elizabeth I gave a ring to her favourite, Robert Devereux, Earl of Essex, saying that if he was ever in trouble and sent the ring back to her, she would come to his aid. When he was awaiting execution in the Tower of London, he sent the ring to Lady Scrope to pass it to the Queen. Unfortunately it was delivered to her sister, the Countess of Nottingham, whose husband was Essex's greatest enemy, and she kept it. On her death-bed she confessed the truth to Elizabeth who, it was said, shook her and exclaimed, 'God may forgive you, but I never can!'

Further to the above: on 14 July 1927 a Mr Earnest Makower presented the Dean of Westminster Abbey with a ring he had recently purchased at Christie's for 520 guineas (£546), believed by many – but not all – to be the memorably historic ring given by Elizabeth to Essex.

After assessing the effects of poison from asps which she had administered to some of her slaves, Cleopatra is believed to have written several books on the subject of women's ailments and venereal diseases.

IN DURANCE VILE

The main London hospital for those suffering mental problems was the Hospital of St Mary of Bethlehem, whose name was abbreviated over the years to Bedlam. It was a popular tourist attraction; one visitor, Samuel Johnson, reported that 'he saw one inmate beating the straw he lay on, supposing it to be William, Duke of Cumberland, whom he was punishing for his cruelties to Scotland.'

Another occupant of Bedlam was Edward Oxford, who spent twenty years there for attempting to assassinate Queen Victoria in June 1840. He was released on condition that he left the country, never to return.

The last naval prison was Bodmin Gaol, Cornwall.

When the renowned prison reformer John Howard visited Germany in 1770 he found that torture was widely practised throughout the country's gaols.

Betty Lou Beets was found guilty and sentenced to death on 14 October 1985 for murdering her husband, but because of the American judicial system remained on Death Row until finally being executed fifteen years later, in 2000.

When Ponchai Wilkerson was being prepared for execution by lethal injection, he surprised the officials by suddenly spitting out a key which would unlock all handcuffs and restraints used in the gaol.

In 1757, £1 was worth about £100 in today's currency, so the fate of a Londoner who, in September of that year, drew the winning ticket for the first prize in a lottery of £10,000, only to have it stolen from him, was understandable; he went mad and had to be confined in an institution.

'Deadman's Hole' is a stone chamber beneath the northern tower of Tower Bridge, in which, in the nineteenth and early twentieth centuries, corpses of those who had committed suicide in the Thames were temporarily deposited after being fished out of the river by yeoman warders on early morning duty.

Dunvegan Castle in the Isle of Skye, founded in the eleventh century, is believed to be the oldest inhabited castle in Scotland.

Judge Sir Richard Adams, who died in 1774, is commemorated by an inscription in Chislehurst church in Kent which reads 'His death was occasioned by the gaol distemper which he caught at the Old Bayly in the Execution of his Office', the distemper being typhus.

John Adam was hanged for murdering his wife in September 1835, and his cadaver buried in an upright position beneath a flagstone in Inverness's Old Gaol.

Mary, Queen of Scots, was once held in Carlisle Castle. The castle's dungeons reportedly contain damp patches, which have been licked so much by the tongues of parched prisoners that there are grooves in the stone.

Louis IX of France not only had the Comte de Nemours executed but ordered that his children should be confined in the Bastille Prison – after first having their teeth pulled out.

The earliest record of a prison is believed to be that in the Book of Genesis, where it is written that Joseph was imprisoned on the false accusation of Potiphar's wife, in about 2000 BC. His confinement was apparently not too intolerable, for 'he found favour in the sight of the keeper of the prison'.

In 1962 three convicts, Frank Morris and the two brothers Anglin, made a daring escape from Alcatraz Island in San Francisco Bay, breaking out and floating to freedom in makeshift boats. They were never seen or heard of again.

A seventeenth-century prisoner in the Tower of London was Sir George Downing, described by Samuel Pepys as an 'ungrateful villain'. Downing supported Cromwell and lured royalists into being arrested and hanged, drawn and quartered, but quickly changed sides when Charles II came to the throne. Known by many of his contemporaries as a traitor and a despicable turncoat, he acquired property in London, built a few brick houses in a cul-de-sac there and named it after himself – Downing Street.

When, in July 1789, the French revolutionary mob stormed the Bastille gaol to release the prisoners, one inmate was an Irishman named Clotworthy Skeffington Massareen, who occupied not a cell but a comfortable apartment on the first floor.

Murderer Tom Tobin was incarcerated in Sing Sing Prison, USA, in the early 1900s. As an ex-mason he was assigned to superintend the construction of new cells and a death house, and he contrived to build a tunnel which connected with a sewer draining into the Hudson River; through this, one night, he escaped. Captured later, after committing another murder, he was sentenced to death in the very room he had designed. 'To think,' he raved, 'that I built this place myself! I built my own tomb, that's what I did!'

Little do the thousands of motorists and pedestrians who cross Tower Bridge daily realise that beneath the northern approach lies the room which was used as the Tower's morgue.

The USA also had a Newgate Prison, an old copper mine in Connecticut, opened in 1773. It was 25 feet below ground, the conditions were appalling and it was closed in 1820.

The execution chambers of most English and Scottish prisons had two entrances. One was a normal-sized doorway through which the sheriff, the clergyman, the prison governor and other official witnesses entered, but the other was at least twice as wide, so that the warders escorting the condemned prisoner could enter while holding his arms.

During efforts by the authorities to restore order after a violent riot in Attica Gaol, New York, in 1971, 39 people were killed and eighty injured.

Refusing to take the Oath of Allegiance to the Crown was definitely frowned on by the courts in July 1624, as James Roche found out when he was sentenced to be imprisoned for life and his possessions forfeited to the King.

Between 1807 and 1899 more than 850,000 Russian convicts were force-marched for distances of five to seven thousand miles, chained together, to imprisonment in Siberia.

Prisoners sentenced to hard labour were made to pick oakum – unpicking short lengths of used rope, having first beaten them against a block of wood. The ropes had to be laboriously unravelled until only thin strands of fibre remained, which would be soaked in tar and used to caulk the decks of ships, i.e., make them watertight by packing it between the planks. Picking oakum resulted in raw and bleeding fingertips, since five pounds of the material was demanded daily from each prisoner.

To have one's head and wrists locked between the boards of the pillory and be exposed to the jeers and sometimes missiles of the spectators was bad enough, but worse could follow, as Timothy Penruddy found out in 1575. Guilty of forgery, he was pilloried in Cheapside, London, on two successive days; on the first day one of his ears was nailed to the wooden frame of the pillory in such a way that he could not move without tearing it from his head; on the second day the other ear had to be sacrificed in the same way.

Because of the unsavoury reputation of America's Sing Sing prison, local residents managed to have the name changed in 1906 to Ossining.

Originally the purpose of prisons was either to change minor criminals' lifestyle in 'Houses of Correction' or to hold 'hardened' criminals pending the arrival of ships in which they would be transported to the colonies. It was not until prisoners could no longer be exiled to America or Australia that prisons became places of detention.

Many newly married couples travel to exotic places to spend their honeymoon alone together, but the Bottle Dungeon at St Andrew's Castle in Scotland would never have been included in any travel firm's brochure. Below ground level, it was seven feet wide at the top, 27 feet wide at its base, and 30 feet deep. In the eighteenth century, when the permission of the laird of the manor was required before marrying, two young people who failed to do so were incarcerated in the Bottle Dungeon for three weeks, on the orders of Simon Fraser, Lord Lovat.

It was reported in the early 1980s that about a third of the young offenders in the Elmira Reformatory, New York, received beatings with a two-foot-long whip, sometimes as often as twice a week.

By the Statute of Winchester (1285) the gates of all walled towns were to be shut from sunset to dawn, and at each gate a watch was to be set to arrest all strangers and suspect travellers, who were then confined in the small towers integral with the gates themselves – hence such ancient gaols as Newgate and others long since demolished.

One of the last public executions in the USA took place in August 1936, when 20,000 spectators crowded round a Kentucky scaffold to watch Rainey Bethea executed.

In 1558 a Protestant heretic named Snell was arrested in Richmond, Yorkshire, and thrown into prison. Eventually, after his toes had rotted off, he agreed to attend Mass, going there on crutches, but he later drowned himself in the nearby River Swail.

Alcatraz – the name means 'Isle of Pelicans' – was discovered in 1775 by the Spanish explorer Manuel de Ayala.

The method by which a convict could summon a prison warder in nineteenth-century and even later gaols was primitive but effective. On his turning a handle in his cell, a gong sounded and a small metal plate outside the cell, bearing the name of the corridor and number of the cell, flipped into a horizontal position, where it was immediately visible to the warder stationed in a central office, from which the corridors radiated like the spokes of a wheel.

Following the adoption of the electric chair as a method of execution in the USA, the judge's pronouncement was 'The sentence of the court is that a current of electricity be passed through your body until you are dead – and may God have mercy on your soul.'

When Britain was at war with America in 1812, nearly three thousand British seamen were held in Dartmoor prison for refusing to obey orders to fight against the American colonists, whom they classed as their own countrymen.

The demolition of old Newgate Gaol (now the site of the Old Bailey Central Criminal Court) commenced on 15 August 1902. The *Daily Mail* described how 'Just below the statue of Liberty on its facade, a piece of stone about the size of a foot fell out on to the pavement, and a hand with a chisel in it was seen working away at it in the breach. The old pigeons, rough and grimy as the prison itself compared with other flocks in London, fluttered about the statue, evidently talking about the event with much excitement. The doom of the gaol was being carried out at last.'

The escaper clambered over the wall, sat down on a nearby bench and scratched his chest thoughtfully. Though he resisted arrest by his keepers, he was overpowered by a narcotic dart and led, swaying drunkenly, back to his cage – because he was a 300lb gorilla named Bokito who went walkabout in Berlin Zoo. Guerrilla warfare was avoided, and there were no casualties.

When, in 1308, the scientist Johannes Scotus was declared dead, his coffin was placed in the family vault in Cologne. Months later, when the vault was opened to admit another coffin, the clerics recoiled in horror on finding the body of Scotus just inside the blood-stained door, his nails broken and fingers fractured in his frantic efforts to escape – in vain.

Tracker dogs, prison warders, police officers, even occasionally teams of soldiers have been employed in recapturing escaped convicts but, when the gaol was in the countryside and the ground was wet and muddy, the task was easier, for the standard-issue prison boots bore studs in the shape of broad arrows, indicating not only that the wanted man had been there but in which direction he was heading.

In the old days, when the accused failed to plead guilty or not guilty, he or she was sentenced to *Peine forte et dure* until pleading one way or the other. The prisoner was tied spreadeagled on his back 'without any Raiment about him, save barely sufficient for decency', with weights on his body 'as much as he can bear, or more; and the next Day following, he shall have three Morsels of Barley Bread, without Drink, and the second Day, he shall have Drink without any Bread; And this shall be his diet till he die.'

Until the practice was abolished by law in 1817, those awaiting hanging in Newgate Gaol attended church service in the prison chapel on the Sunday prior to their executions. They were seated in an open pew, the prison officials and all the other convicts being present. The service was taken by the Ordinary, the prison chaplain, and, as a morbid reminder of the occasion, a black painted coffin rested on a table in the centre of the hall throughout the proceedings.

Only yards from the entrance to the Tower of London stands a small circular kiosk-type structure, which until the end of the nineteenth century was an entrance to one of the earliest tunnels under the River Thames. Constructed in 1869, about seven feet in diameter, it could be said to be the city's first Tube, a cable-operated 'omnibus' transported fourteen passengers at a time to a similar station on the south bank of the river. Within a few years, however, it was converted for use by foot-passengers only, an eerie journey hardly enhanced by the sound of the engines of the paddle steamers passing overhead. Eventually closed, it now carries pipelines, conduits and cables and, as the author can personally testify, just to peer down into its depths is something of a spine-chilling experience!

In 1721 highwayman William Spiggott, sentenced to *Peine forte et dure* to make him plead guilty or not guilty, managed to resist the appalling pressure of 350lb on his chest for half an hour, but gave in when a further 50lb were added. Then they found him guilty and hanged him.

The eighteenth-century prison reformer John Howard recommended to the authorities that all prison cell walls should be whitewashed, not for reasons of hygiene but so that any attempts by the cell's occupant to escape by scraping away the bricks and mortar would be instantly obvious.

In pre-union days, George Loveless, the leader of the Tolpuddle Martyrs, who in 1834 went on strike for higher wages, was sentenced to seven years transportation in Australia, together with many of his fellow workers.

Alcatraz Prison closed in 1963 and is now a popular tourist attraction.

During the Napoleonic Wars of the early 1800s, French prisoners of war were held in Dartmoor prison, and many tried to escape and return to France. During one such attempt, some tunnelled for many months before eventually making a successful getaway. They reported that they had found themselves in a cave containing many bones and skeletons, together with pieces of Roman armour.

TRADITIONS AND SUPERSTITIONS

Men's coats fasten left over right so that they (if right-handed!) can draw their swords; women's coats fasten right over left so that, if 'having a child at breast', they can suppport the infant with their left hand and continue working in the fields or the kitchen on tasks requiring the right hand.

An old tradition in Haiti holds that if a zombie is given even a grain of salt, it will break the sorcerer's spell over him, and he will realise that he is a walking corpse without a grave – with indescribably horrific results!

At his execution in 1821, John Davies claimed he had been wrongly accused of robbery and declared on the scaffold that, as proof of his innocence, no grass would ever grow on his grave. Nor did it, for in the Montgomery churchyard where he lies buried the earth is bare, despite being frequently resown.

Because of their dangerous way of life, sailors were understandably superstitious. One way in which they believed they could avoid bad luck was never to hand the ship's flag to another through the rungs of a ladder.

St Valentine is regarded as the patron saint of lovers, but he is also the patron saint of people suffering from even more devastating afflictions – epilepsy and the plague.

The number seven was believed by the ancients to have extra-magical qualities, so to have it in one's car registration number is a bonus, especially if the registration also includes the letter U – because of its resemblance to a lucky horseshoe. Doubtless to have 777 UUU would remove the need for motor insurance altogether!

More than ten million 'lucky' rabbit-foot charms are sold in the USA each year.

In Wyoming, the Medicine Wheel of the Big Horn Mountains has baffled all researchers. It consists of a circle of stone 70 feet in diameter, with 28 stone 'spokes' connecting the 12-foot-diameter hub, which has a seven-foot opening in its centre. Its purpose has never been established.

'Carat', a measure of the value of precious stones, is derived from the Greek word for the seeds of the locust tree fruit, which, being of uniform weight, were used by Orientals to weigh small articles. Approximately 150 carats equal 1 ounce.

A US Navy pilot of American Indian descent was flying his aircraft in the sinister Bermuda Triangle, lost contact with base and disappeared without trace. The last sound heard over the intercom was him singing a song which was identified by other American Indians listening in as the 'death song', to be sung just before one's death and at no other time.

Children with rickets used to be taken and laid on the Nancledra Stone near St Ives, Cornwall; if it rocked, they were healed – but if they were illegitimate, it didn't!

The nursery rhyme 'Oranges and lemons, say the bells of St Clement's' is believed to have originated in the old days when the

Thames was not only the City's sewer but a route for barges, which landed their cargoes below the bridge, baskets of fruit were then carried through Clement's Inn to Clare Market. Because of the disturbance this traffic caused to the tenants of the Inn, toll was at first exacted, but this was replaced by pieces of fruit, namely oranges and lemons, being given every New Year's Day.

Covering 600 acres of prairie near Mount Shasta in the north-western USA are a large number of circular mounds, sixty feet in diameter, raised two feet above the level of the surrounding earth. Each mound is encircled by an arrangement of large stones on top of smaller ones. Whether these were created for religious or sacrificial ceremonies has never been established.

A book of etiquette published in Melbourne in 1886 urged that the traditional bathing-dress material for ladies should be flannel, with a belted waist and reaching halfway down the thigh (to use a forbidden word!). Matching socks should be worn and, as the hair had at all costs to remain dry, an oilskin cap was essential.

The patron saint of young virgins is St Agnes; her Feast Day is 21 January.

A Yorkshire superstition involved riddling the chaff on St Mark's Eve. If at midnight two persons were seen to glide past the barn door, the one who was riddling would die within the year.

Crossing one's fingers to avert evil is, of course, literally making a sign of the Cross.

'Shires', the ancient divisions of England, were controlled by offi-cials known as 'reeves', the name 'shire-reeve' eventually becoming 'sheriff'; the term was introduced into America by the early English colonists.

Precious stones were always credited with having magical powers; carbuncles neutralised poisons, jasper cured fevers, agate improved eyesight, carnelian stopped haemorrhages.

Gentlemen in the eighteenth century were warned not to use the expression 'old hat', as it is a nickname in some circles 'for a woman's privities'.

To stand in the centre of the eye of the chalk White Horse of Uffingham is not only lucky but a guarantee that one's wishes will come true.

Even though garden gnomes spend all their time in the garden, there is no truth in the theory that the letters GNOME stand for Guardians Naturally Over Mother Earth!

A three-hundred-year-old trumpet, reputed to bring its owner bad luck if not blown frequently, was auctioned at Christie's in 1967. A musician blew a fanfare to start the bidding, and the instrument was ultimately sold for £1,600.

There is an ancient belief that ringing sounds heard near the Blackpool shore come from the bells of the submerged church of Kilgrimol.

A survey in 1965 discovered that some mothers, believing the smell of gas would cure their children's whooping cough, walked their offspring three times round the local gasworks.

In Holland, in recent centuries, whenever the funeral of a local resident was taking place, the village's miller would show his respects by slowly rotating that section of his windmill bearing the sails to face the solemn cortege as it wended its way towards the church.

The language of fans, as used by Georgian ladies, included holding the tip to the nose – 'you are not to be trusted'; chin on tip – 'your flattery annoys me'; and tip to forehead – 'you are out of your mind.' Perforce, men had to carry a code-book!

The words 'diamond' in English and 'diamant' in French are synonymous with 'adamant', which comes from a Greek word meaning 'hard', 'untameable' or 'unconquerable'.

In 1538 every priest had to maintain a register of births and deaths. Because the Bishop of London controlled the chaplains of English ships, children born and baptised on ships afloat were registered by him and recorded in the books of St Dunstan's church in Stepney. So it was said that all babies born at sea were parishioners of that Borough. This system changed in 1837 when civil registration was instituted.

When a member of a farmer's family dies, the rural custom of informing the cattle should be observed; any bees kept should also be told, specifically by the eldest son, who must first tap on the hive three times and make the announcement, otherwise the bees will leave the hive and not return.

People passing the ravens' cages in the Tower of London after dusk have been known to bid the birds goodnight – and to receive a similar reply. Ravens and birds of similar species are excellent mimics, but so far as is known, no members of the Tower's unkindness of ravens have been heard to insist that they are innocent prisoners and demand to see a feathered lawyer (an owl?).

So old is the area around Fleet Street, it is believed that the extensive vaults underneath the famous Cheshire Cheese Tavern were part of some mediaeval religious priory.

Charles the Bold, Duke of Burgundy, owned the 133-carat Florentine Diamond and always took it with him into battle for luck. It let him down, however, at Morat in June 1476, when he lost both the battle and the gem.

To 'ride the high toby' in the eighteenth century was to adopt the profession of highwayman.

Saint Bartholomew was martyred by being flayed alive, his skin slowly peeled off in strips. A statue of him carrying a knife and a length of his own skin graces a square in Milan.

In some rural counties local superstition states that a corpse must never be left alone in a house, so someone should always remain with it and stay awake.

There is no record of capital punishment in England earlier than 450 BC. The method of execution at that time was being thrown into a quagmire.

The origin of the street name 'St Mary Axe', off Bishopsgate, is believed to stem from the *Chronicles* of St Matthew of Westminster, in which, under the date AD 393, he described how 'Eleven thousand virgins fell in with the lawless army of Wannius, king of the Huns; the soldiers, meeting with these damsels and beholding their beauty, desired to wanton with them, but when the damsels refused, and had, in a most Christian spirit, looked with due disdain on the pagans, the soldiers rushed on them, the chaste band being cut to pieces, and went to the kingdom of heaven as martyrs.' A church, since demolished, was built in that

London thoroughfare and, after being dedicated to St Mary, acquired one of the axes reportedly used in the massacre.

A century or so ago, it was recommended that the best way to remove the odour of smoking from the breath was to chew a leaf or two of parsley.

The boundary between the Cities of London and Westminster on Fleet Street, where royalty, on wishing to enter the City of London, must halt and touch the hilt of the Pearl Sword offered by the Lord Mayor, used to be marked by Temple Bar, an elegant stone gate or archway designed by Sir Christopher Wren and built in 1670/72. At one time ornamented by the heads of traitors, it was dismantled in 1877 because of increased traffic, and now, although classified as an ancient monument, stands piecemeal, forlorn and neglected in Theobalds Park, Herefordshire. What a pity.

The reason for wearing dark clothing after a funeral is assumed to be to show respect for the deceased, but some believe it is a means of disguising oneself from ghosts and so avoiding being haunted.

Under the Roman law of the Twelve Tables (451–450 BC) many crimes carried the death sentence, such as publishing insulting songs, wilful murder of a parent and making disturbances in the city at night.

In Victorian days, a housemaid was known as a 'mop-squeezer' or a 'sixpounder', the latter term derived from her usual annual wages.

Confusion exists between ducking stools and cucking stools. A ducking stool was a chair on the end of a type of see-saw, which was lowered into a village pond or river to cure a nagging woman. A cucking stool was a toilet-shaped seat (the name being derived from *cathedra stercoris*, from the Greek *kathedra*, seat, and the Latin *stercus*, dung) on which the culprit had to sit, as a humiliating penalty, outside their own front door.

As a warning to gentlemen who were going bald, the Victorians advised the wearing of straw 'boaters' instead of silk top-hats.

Those responsible for the French Revolution decided not only to change society but to introduce a different calendar as well. Some of the names for the new months were Germinal (month of buds), 22 March–20 April; Prairial (month of meadows), 21 May–19 June; Frumaire (month of frosts), 22 November–21 December; and Brumaire (month of mists), 23 October–21 November. Poetic maybe, but they didn't last.

As explained in more detail elsewhere, high treason was the crime of conspiring to kill, or actually killing, the sovereign, the leader of the 'family' of the nation; low, petit, or petty treason was the crime committed by a woman who killed the leader of her family, her husband. The charge did not apply to husbands who killed their wives.

After the Monmouth Rebellion of 1685 Judge Jeffries, the hanging judge, was renowned for the cruel sentences he handed down. In the area where most of the rebel army had lived, 'the pitch cauldron was constantly boiling, and the heads and limbs preserved in it were distributed over the lovely west country, frightening the village labourer as he passed to his cottage in the evening. And the peasant who had poured the pitch over the severed heads and limbs became known throughout the county as William Boilman.'

A traditional cure to remove freckles in the days of Queen Victoria was to apply a lotion consisting of an ounce of honey diluted in a pint of warm water.

In his will, Robert Dow, who died in 1612, left '26s 8d yearly for ever' for the sexton or bellman of St Sepulchre's church by Newgate (now the Old Bailey) to toll the passing bell on the eve of an execution and to exhort those condemned to confess their sins. The bell is still displayed within the church, its clapper now permanently silenced.

Many grimly apt sayings have been used to describe the act of being hanged; among them were 'to go to rest in a horse's night-cap' (halter), or 'to be stabbed by a Bridport dagger' (a Dorset town where hempen rope was made). The writhing victim was also said to have 'danced at the Sheriff's Ball and stuck his tongue out at the company'. The entire operation was described as 'to be scragged, ottomised, and then grin in a glass case' – to be hanged, anatomised (dissected) and have one's skeleton displayed in Surgeons' Hall.

The tradition whereby felons en route to Tyburn stopped at 'The Bowl' for a last drink – 'one for the road' – was abolished on 7 February 1750. Some years earlier a Captain Stafford, his morale undiminished, asked mine host for a bottle of wine, saying that while he had an appointment to keep, he would pay the landlord on the way back!

'Reading the Riot Act' to unruly children is based on a statutory tradition which existed until comparatively recent times. Should a gathering of twelve or more people appear to be potentially violent or causing excessive disturbance, a Justice of the Peace would read the Riot Act to them 'in a loud voice', warning them that if they failed to disperse within one hour, they would be classed as criminals, and be subject to the Law. In extreme cases, armed police or even the military could be called out.

The significance of receiving the accolade, i.e., being knighted by having one's shoulders touched by the sword, is that having received a gift (of knighthood), one should now expect similar blows in the service of the giver.

To appear sunburned in Edwardian society was frowned upon, but fortunately the unwanted hue could be removed by applying a mixture of two drams of borax, one of alum and one of camphor, together with an ounce of sugar-candy and a pound of ox-gall, well-stirred, and then strained through blotting paper.

The traditional sentence in Scotland for cursing one's parents and murdering either of them was passed on Philip Standsfield in 1688, the judge stating that 'he was to be hanged until he be dead, his tongue to be cut out and burnt upon the scaffold [for cursing his father], his right hand to be cut off [which struck the blow] and affixed on the East Port of Haddington, and his body taken and hanged on the gibbet; his name, fame, memory and honours were then to be made extinct, and his coat of arms to be riven forth and deleted out of the book of arms.'

Andrew Mills was hanged in Durham in 1683 for killing his master's three children, and his corpse was exhibited on the local gibbet. Long after the body had disintegrated, part of the wooden gibbet remained, bits of it having been taken away to wear as traditional charms to ward off toothache.

If you had lived in the eighteenth century and counterfeited the stamps used for the sale of perfumery and hair powder, or robbed a rabbit warren, or impersonated a Greenwich Pensioner, you would have committed a capital offence and been hanged.

The buildings of mediaeval towns were usually made of wood, sometimes thatched, with primitive chimneys; devastating fires frequently consumed whole streets and even towns. To reduce this risk a nightly curfew bell was rung – the word originating with the French *couvre feu*, cover fire – warning residents to extinguish fires with a pan-shaped utensil. The only curfew bell still sounded in London is in the Tower of London; installed centuries ago in the Bell Tower, it is now rung each evening by the Yeoman Warder Watchman, to indicate to visitors that it is time for them to leave. In earlier centuries, when many prisoners were allowed to have their servants attend to their needs, the curfew bell warned the servants to vacate the Tower.

In Victorian days, if one called upon an acquaintance and had to wait in the music room, one was required to remember one's manners and never try a few notes on the piano, or examine family pictures or ornaments, but simply stand and muse.

The *Gentleman's Magazine* of October 1757 included an item describing how 'at the interment of Mr Cambden at St James Church, Shadwell, minute guns were fired from the good ship *Happy Return* [moored in the Thames not far away] as a traditional tribute. The guns, however, not being properly examined, one was fired with two balls in the barrel, one of which went through a house, and in it cut through the sacking and tick of a bed on which lay an exciseman very ill. It did not hurt him, other than by frightening him much, to find himself buried in loose feathers on the floor. The other cannon ball went through three rooms in another house without doing any further damage than much frightening the neighbours.'

The belief that the effigies of knights lying on tombs with their legs crossed signified that they went on the Crusades against the infidels would appear to be erroneous. There is an effigy of a cross-legged woman in a church in Howden, Yorkshire, and another on the tomb of Sir Fulk FitzWarin, one of the Knights of the Garter.

Different flowers mean different things to people. The Victorians traditionally assigned varying sentiments to blooms: Acacia signified concealed love; Anemone, expectation; Arum, ardour; and Coreopsis, love at first sight. But other, less sentimental messages could also be florally conveyed: Basil for hatred; Bilberry, treachery; Pik China, aversion, and Coltsfoot, justice shall be done to you.

The Yeoman Warders of the Tower of London, the 'Beefeaters', are the longest serving uniformed body of men in the world still carrying out the duties for which they were originally formed – guarding the Tower and all who live within its walls.

In the Middle Ages, when a crime had been committed in a shire, the 'Hue and Cry' would be raised; the inhabitants would cause an outcry, shouting to summon neighbours, and all would chase the criminal(s) to the shire boundary. The cry was then taken up by those who lived in the adjoining shire.

DISASTERS, GREAT AND SMALL

Shipping losses due to enemy action during World War I were appalling. During 1917, 2,734 British vessels were sunk, and a quarter of those sailing from the UK never returned. On the other hand, during World War II, nearly 1,100 enemy ships sank after striking British mines.

During a storm in southern England in November 1703, 700 sailing ships in London's docklands were blown from their moorings and some were sunk, as were 500 barges; 300 seamen, bargees, lightermen and wharfingers were drowned, twelve warships and scores of merchant ships along the coast sank, in all 18,000 men perished. Thousands of houses in the City were damaged or demolished, including some of the historic Tudor dwellings within the Tower of London.

2,539 people died of bubonic plague in England during the week ending 25 August 1603 and a further 3,025 in the week after. The total number of casualties for that year was 30,578, plus 500 dogs in Westminster, which were thought to be the carriers of the disease; their corpses were buried at least four feet deep. The disease was actually carried by rat fleas.

When the Irish Fenians blew up the Clerkenwell House of Detention on 13 December 1867 in an attempt to free some of their colleagues, the consequences were vividly described in *The Times* of 29 April 1868. 'Six persons were killed outright, six more died from its effects. In addition, five owed their deaths indirectly to the outrage; one young woman is in a madhouse, forty women were prematurely confined and twenty of their babies died from the effects of the explosion on the women; others of the children are dwarfed and unhealthy. One mother is now a raving lunatic; one hundred and twenty persons were wounded; fifty went into St Bart's, Gray's Inn Lane and King's College Hospitals; fifteen are permanently injured, with the loss of eyes, legs, arms, etc., besides twenty thousand pounds worth of damage to person and property.'

During the cholera epidemic of 1849, victims assumed to be dead were quickly put into coffins so that living ones could be attended to. Sometimes however, knocking would be heard from the coffins, 'but we never opened them up, because we knew they were going to die anyway!' quoth one woman in charge of the epidemic wards.

In September 1792 burglars broke into the Garde-Meuble in Paris and stole the French Crown Jewels and other national treasures. Most were later recovered. Some of the thieves were condemned to the galleys, others to prison, where they eventually died.

Many more spectators than usual attended the gruesome entertainment on 23 February 1807, when the murderers Holloway and Haggerty were due for the drop. The street outside the Old Bailey was packed when, just before the felons appeared, panic broke out, people fighting and struggling to avoid being crushed. When the police cleared the area, thirty persons lay dead and many others injured.

The British Army was forever fighting during Queen Victoria's reign, first in Afghanistan, then the Punjab; in Burma in 1852 and

1885; the Crimean War in 1854; the Indian Mutiny in 1857. Trouble in Ashanti, now Ghana, flared in 1873 and 1895, and still more in Zululand, South Africa, in 1879. The year 1899 saw our troops fighting the Boers; 1901, the Chinese in the Boxer Rebellion. Any more for the Queen's Shilling?

Many people in Eyam, Derbyshire, contracted the plague in 1665, so the residents heroically decided to remain in the village to prevent spreading the disease. Food was sent by the Earl of Devonshire and left on a stone on the parish boundary. Out of a population of 350, 260 died.

The collapse of a mountainous slagheap of coal sludge overlooking a school in the Welsh town of Aberfan on 21 October 1966 killed 144 people, 116 of them children in the classrooms.

Some contemporary historians reported that the Great Fire of London started in Pudding Lane and burnt itself out at Pie Corner.

During the Massacre of Nishapur in 1269, 1,747,000 people were reportedly slain on the orders of Genghis Khan; it took twelve days to count the corpses.

The Spanish influenza outbreak in 1918 brought agonising death to between 20 and 40 million people, a sixtieth of the world's population.

In the mysterious and apparently deadly Bermuda Triangle off the east coast of America, thousands of ships have disappeared over the centuries, with no wreckage subsequently discovered; on other occasions only the passengers have vanished, and the vessels found abandoned. Aircraft too have disappeared without trace; in December 1945 not only did a flight of five

Avenger bombers vanish, but also the rescue plane sent to assist them.

Following the tsunami earthquake catastrophe in December 2004, scientists calculated that the Earth wobbled on its axis by an inch or more, and cut the length of a day by a few millionths of a second.

On 27 March 1977, a jumbo jet carrying 248 passengers was taking off from Tenerife when it slammed into a jumbo jet, with 380 people aboard, on the runway; 583 were killed.

In the North African desert region in 1658 a 'pestilential blast', reportedly about twenty yards in breadth and travelling twelve feet above the ground, suffocated 20,000 men in one night. In the desert, on seeing the distant purplish haze approaching, people threw themselves down and wrapped their heads in their robes, while their camels and horses buried their nostrils in the sand. At first, those killed by the blast appeared to be asleep, 'but if an arm or a leg be smartly shaken or lifted up, it separates from the body, which soon after becomes black'.

During a storm in 1236, boats were rowed into Westminster Hall, which had been flooded by the Thames's unexpectedly high tide.

On the evening of 16 October 1834 a devastating fire broke out in the House of Lords, which spread rapidly and was not extinguished for several days. Nothing was left of either the House of Lords or the House of Commons except bare walls. It was started when two cart-loads of Exchequer tallies (engraved strips of wood used to count and calculate Government funds) were being burnt in the furnaces, the flues of which passed beneath the wooden floors of the House of Lords and ignited them.

Nearly ten thousand people in England were killed in 1783 by the toxic fumes emitted by an erupting volcano in Iceland.

An appalling explosion occurred on 4 January 1649, near the Tower of London, caused by a ships' chandler while he was barrelling gunpowder. Fifty or sixty houses were demolished, including the Rose Tavern and those partaking of the parish dinner therein. After digging in the ruins, men discovered the landlady of the inn, sitting in her bar, and one of the barmen standing nearby with a pot of beer in his hand; although the falling roof timbers had prevented them from being crushed, both had been suffocated by the dust and smoke.

In 1556 an earthquake in China killed 830,000 people.

The Great Fire decimated London in 1666; in 1667 the Dutch fleet sailed up the river Medway and destroyed most of the English fleet.

The Black Death, which arrived in Europe in the fourteenth century, killed 25 million people in the following three hundred years. London's death roll in 1665 totalled 100,000 victims.

Not a ghastly disaster – yet! On 6 August 1944 an American cargo ship, the *Robert Montgomery*, ran aground on the Sheerness Sands in a gale; it now lies 28 feet down, less than two miles off the town of Sheerness. The vessel's cargo consisted of 8,687 tons of bombs and detonators, now all heavily corroded. The wreck is categorised as an extreme hazard, should a passing ship happen to collide with it . . .

The labyrinth of tunnels with which the Rock of Gibraltar is honeycombed is believed by many to be haunted by the ghosts of servicemen who were killed during the construction of the miles of passages over the last two and a half centuries.

Following reports over many years of supernatural happenings in the Devonport naval base in Plymouth, in 2004 paranormal researchers investigated the sightings of a ghostly young girl in one house and a bearded sailor clad in eighteenth-century naval rig elsewhere in the grounds. One particular location requiring their attention was the Hangman's Cell, where more than a hundred men have been executed.

During the Black Death of 1347, thirteen million people died in China. The Tartars, who at that time were invading Turkey, took ghastly advantage of the appalling plague: while besieging the town of Caffa, they infected the defenders by 'firing' putrefying bodies over the walls with trebuchets, giant catapults made of wood.

One of the most memorable earthquakes in English history occurred on 8 February 1750, when, according to Horace Walpole, 'a shock was felt, followed exactly one month later by a second and severer one, when all the bells of the church clocks in the swaying spires struck against the chiming-hammers, dogs howled, and fish jumped high out of the water.'

The residents of Lambeth were so incensed in 1832 at the absence of proper sewerage during the plague epidemic that was killing thousands that they threatened the authorities 'with the Halter and the Lamp-iron' – a rope slung over a street-lamp bracket and tightened.

Horatio Nelson went into battle at Trafalgar wearing his full admiral's uniform, thereby presenting a perfect target for enemy snipers aboard the French ships. Risking his displeasure, his officers asked him to wear a less conspicuous uniform or cover his decorations, but Nelson reminded his officers that he had won them with honour, and would wear them until he died. He was indeed fired at, a musket shot from the *Redoubtable* striking him in the chest, penetrating his spine and fatally wounding him. His last words were, 'I have done my duty, thank God for that.'

James IV of Scotland wanted to lead his army at the Battle of Flodden Field in 1513 but realised that dressed as a king he would make a perfect target for the English, so several of his knights were ordered to wear royal apparel as well. It didn't help him, though, for both he and his stand-ins were killed in the fighting.

Surprisingly, women served aboard warships in Nelson's day. A gunner on HMS *Goliath* during the Battle of the Nile in 1798 described how, being below decks and not knowing how the battle topside was going, 'Any information we got from the boys and the women who brought the powder for our guns. They behaved as well as the men, and got a prize for their bravery later. I was much indebted to the gunner's wife who gave her husband and me a drink of wine every now and then, which lessened our fatigue much. There were some of the women wounded, and one woman from Leith died of her wounds, and was buried on a small island in the bay. One woman bore a son in the heat of the action; she belonged to Edinburgh.'

Further to the above: the phrase 'Show a leg!' was originally used to rouse sailors asleep in hammocks. The bosun giving the order would then survey the proffered leg; if it was smooth and slender, he would not bother the lady further, but if the limb was hairy and muscular, he would expect its owner to hit the deck forthwith.

To sailors, plovers, curlews, and any birds that emitted a plaintive whistle were known as the 'Seven Whistlers'; should they be heard flying near a ship, maritime misfortune would surely follow.

A catastrophic train crash, in which nearly five hundred people, mostly soldiers, were killed, occurred on 22 May 1915, when a packed troop train collided at speed with a stationary local train at Quintinshill, north of Carlisle. The wreckage was then struck by the Glasgow express travelling at 60mph.

William IV once sailed out in the Royal Yacht and ordered the warships moored in Portsmouth to follow him. They obeyed but, not having been informed of their destination, for His Majesty did not have one in mind, they sailed around for a while and then returned to harbour.

In 1942 the liner *Queen Mary*, carrying 15,000 troops to England, suddenly changed course following a U-boat warning and collided with the escort cruiser HMS *Curacao*, cutting it in half; 25 officers and 313 seamen were drowned.

Karl Lody, a German spy shot by firing squad on 6 November 1914, was the first man to be executed in the Tower of London for 150 years.

Wilhelm Fabry, a sixteenth-century German surgeon, prescribed a curative dressing for those who had suffered severe sword wounds in battle; it consisted of earthworms, swine's brains, human mummy, powdered lodestone and moss from the skull of a hanged man. This was applied, not to the wound but to the weapon that had inflicted it, a fresh dressing being prepared each day. In most cases this worked and the wound healed successfully, probably because the medical men were concentrating on the weapon rather than messing about with the wound.

Press-gangs, who kidnapped men for service in the Navy in the eighteenth century, even attempted to seize a bridegroom at his wedding, but the vicar and churchwardens defended him so vigorously that he – and his bride – escaped.

In 1917 a black girl in Texas was arrested by a policeman and, when a black soldier intervened, a fight started, resulting in soldiers from the local barracks arming themselves and joining in. So violent was the rioting which followed that some civilians were killed, and as a consequence thirteen soldiers of the US Army's 24th Infantry were hanged simultaneously.

The enemy spies executed for treason during World War I were buried in the East London Cemetery at Plaistow.

As amulets against drowning, sailors of old would wear gold earrings. Some even believed that carrying a caul, the membrane that covers a baby's head at birth, would protect them from a watery grave.

In 1958 a bomb fell on Naples which was identified as having been manufactured in 1942 and being of the type dropped over Italy during World War II. No trace was found of the aircraft presumably responsible.

Adolf Hitler was a firm believer in omens, especially the number seven. Because Sunday is counted as the seventh day of the week, during World War II he launched his major attacks on Austria, Russia, Greece, Poland, Holland and Yugoslavia on that day.

On 4 October 1930 the giant airship R101, 200 yards in length, had developed so many technical faults during its construction that en route to India it went out of control, eventually crashing in France with the loss of 48 passengers and crew, including Lord Thomson, the Minister for Air.

J. Kincaid, in his book *Adventures in the Rifle Brigade*, published in 1838, about his experiences fighting in the Napoleonic wars in Spain in 1810–11, described how, 'during a truce with the enemy, repeated acts of civility passed between the French and us. The greyhound owned by one of our officers followed a hare on one occasion, ran into the enemy lines, and they very politely returned the dog to us. On another occasion I was on sentry duty one night when a ball [bullet] came from the French sentry and struck the burning logs of wood round which we were sitting, and they sent a flag of truce next morning, to apologise for the action, saying that it had been done by a stupid fellow of a sentry who had imagined that we were advancing on him!'

A 'Dear John' letter, received by a serviceman while serving abroad during World War II, was one from a wife or girlfriend saying that she had found companionship elsewhere. The recipient was not, of course, permitted to return home to attempt a reconciliation.

When Tower Bridge was being designed in the late nineteenth century, not only had its appearance to blend in with that of the Tower of London, but the military authorities stipulated that provision should be made for soldiers to be stationed on the tops of its towers for defensive purposes, if necessary. The latter demand was far-sighted, for an anti-aircraft battery was positioned there during World War II to engage enemy bombers using the Thames as an unmistakable route from the coast into the heart of the capital.

In the cemetery of St Mary's parish church in the village of Great Sankey, Cheshire, lie the remains of Sergeant Donaghue, who blew the bugle call which launched the disastrous Charge of the Light Brigade in the Crimean War.

In Canada in 1945 four German prisoners of war were hanged for having murdered a fellow inmate; a further seven were similarly executed in Fort Leavenworth, Kansas, USA, for killing another POW whom they had accused of being a traitor to the German Reich.

In Tudor times, when wars raged, ordinary ships were commandeered and moored at Tower Wharf, where they were fitted out with forecastles and after-castles to be manned by archers; guns, manufactured in the Tower were installed, and the words 'of the Tower' added to the name of the ship. After hostilities, the equipment and additional names were removed and the ships resumed their normal occupation.

During World War II tens of thousands of servicemen and women were transported abroad to the various theatres of war in troopships, which were hastily converted merchant ships. Herded into the bowels of these vessels, aware of the continuous threat of torpedo attacks by the U-boats lying in wait, they faced ever-present danger. Their duties included manning the watertight doors separating the various holds; if the ship was attacked, the orders were to close and lock the doors immediately, to preserve buoyancy – but one never knew which side of the doors the torpedo had struck.

A sixteenth-century surgeon, Ambroise Par, in the town of Metz during a siege, realised the desperate need for clean bandages with which to bind wounds and reused old ones 'having them washed by four fat prostitutes'. The result was far from perfect, but understandable, seeing that, as the surgeon admitted, 'there was no water available and less soap!'

WITCH WAY TO DIE

The word 'witchcraft' is derived from the Old English word *wiccian*, meaning to practise sorcery, to harness evil spirits for occult purposes.

In 1582 thirteen witches were hanged in Essex.

In the Caribbean, whenever UFOs (Unidentified Flying Objects) had been seen in the area, 'miracles' were reported such as tears appearing on the cheeks of church statues, and amazing cures of fatally ill people.

To bring ill-luck or misfortune to an enemy, Australian Aborigines would cast a spell while pointing a sharp bone at them.

Women weren't the only ones persecuted for witchcraft; *The Times* of 24 September 1863 gave a detailed account of an old man in Essex being mobbed to death as a wizard.

Romanian Petre Toma was believed by the residents of his village to be a vampire. After his death in 2003 they swore that his undead cadaver sucked their blood – so they dug him up and tore his heart out.

The ancient Egyptians frequently laid curses which would have dire results should anyone break into their tombs. This gave some credence to the rumour that a mummy had been part of the cargo in the hold of the ill-fated *Titanic*.

Margaret Harris, who was executed for murder in 1883, had once tried to kill a woman by filling a bottle with water and some white beans, then burying it upside down in the ground. As the beans germinated and swelled, so the woman would similarly swell and be ill; when the bottle eventually burst, the woman would also. The spell failed, so Harris resorted to using poison instead.

Nearly fifty witches were executed, most of them burned at the stake, between 1603 and 1618, during the reign of James I.

The world's largest collection of witchcraft artefacts, memorabilia and books is contained in the Museum of Witchcraft in Boscastle, Cornwall. The museum was severely damaged by flash floods in August 2004, but reopened in 2005.

In 1441 the Duchess of Gloucester was accused of consorting with other witches to make a waxen image of Henry VI, then joining in the accompanying incantations as it melted before the fire, a procedure which would result in the King slowly dying. She was made to walk through jeering crowds in the London streets and was then imprisoned in Peel Castle in the Isle of Man until her death in 1454.

When cases of witchcraft were being investigated in the seventeenth century in the Channel Islands, torture was permitted and frequently applied.

Following the witchcraft trials in Salem, Massachusetts, in 1692, nineteen innocent people were hanged.

Vampires were always buried at crossroads, so that, should they revive, they would not know which road led them back to their homes.

In 1947 an Army pensioner assaulted a woman who, he declared, had attempted to bewitch him with a bunch of flowers.

'Hex' means to bewitch, or an evil spell, or a witch. The word comes via Pennsylvanian Dutch from the German *Hexe*, a witch.

Crosses made of rowan wood were guaranteed to safeguard one's cattle from a witch's spells.

A Voodoo man is called a 'Hungan', his female counterpart a 'Mambo'. Their meeting place is a 'Humfo', their 'patients' are known as 'hunsi' and the medicine is 'Loa', the guiding spirit.

Gilles de Rais, one of the most sadistic warlocks in fourteenth-century France, tortured and disembowelled young children during Satanic ceremonies. After his death, the skulls and bones of more than two hundred of them were dredged up from the moat of his castle.

Legend has it that Warwickshire witch covens frequently met at dead of night at the Rollright Stones near the crest of the Cotswold Hills; it is also said that because of a spell, the stones cannot be counted twice alike.

In the seventeenth century some Scottish witches were led to execution wearing a 'Witch's Brank', an iron-framed cage locked about the head. It incorporated a spiked mouthpiece which pressed down on the tongue to prevent the wearer from either summoning the devil to free her or intoning a curse on her captors.

The word *incubus*, the male demon that has intimacy with sleeping women, comes from the Latin *incubare*, meaning to lie on; *succubus*, the female demon which has intimacy with sleeping men, derives from the Latin *succubare*, to lie beneath.

Sir Robert Tresilian, Lord Chief Justice to Richard II, was found guilty of treason and hanged. He was then stripped 'and certain Images were found on him, like the Signs in the Heavens, and the head of a Devil painted, and the names of many Devils written in Parchment; and he was hanged naked for some time and then his Throat was cut and his Body given to his wife for burial in Grey-Friars.'

Among the Stiperstones in Shropshire is one called the Devil's Chair, in which he presided over meetings of local witches. It is said that should anyone sit in it now, a storm would immediately spring up.

A Haitian zombie is brought to 'life' by a sorcerer who wafts a bottle containing its soul under its nose and so brings it under his spell.

In ancient Persia the sisters of Simeon, the Christian bishop of Salencia, were found guilty of using witchcraft to make the Empress ill, and so were sawn in quarters while still alive; their body-parts were tied to posts, between which the Empress passed, as charms to cure her.

It is believed that the earliest known 'swimming' test, to determine whether a person was a witch or not, took place in Babylon in 2250 BC.

Eighteen witches were put to death at Bury St Edmunds in one day, 27 August 1645.

The law against witchcraft in Victoria, Australia, was obviously ineffective; when the statute was abolished in 2003, more than two thousand self-confessed witches were still living there.

During the Middle Ages some Scottish witches in the north-east were rolled down Cluny Hill, Forres, in internally spiked barrels, which, together with the torn remains of the occupants, were then burned on the Witches' Stone at the foot of the hill.

In Haiti, some peasants bury their dead relatives face down, in the belief that they will not hear the dreaded call of the sorcerer.

Margery Wilson was found guilty on 10 December 1599 of bewitching Mary Rust and Bridget Bruer 'so that they languished and died'; she also bewitched a cow, valued at £2, to death. She was hanged forthwith.

The Ironmongers' Company had an article printed in every issue of the annual *Dictionary of London* between 1879 and 1894. The article was headed by a passage which read: 'In the Company's Hall is a portrait of members, which includes Mr John Nicholl. This worthy person bequeathed to the Company a sum of money, the interest of which was to be spent in the purchase of faggots [bundles of twigs bound together and used as fuel] for the burning of witches. Nowadays the Ironmongers do not advocate extreme measures, and the money is now devoted to the warming, not the burning, of the poor.'

In February 1960 more than a dozen women in Monteros, Argentina, woke up screaming on finding a man biting their throats and sucking their blood. The 'vampire' turned out to be 25-year-old Florenico Fernandez, who admitted that he was unable to resist such appalling impulses.

Some reports state that Ipswich was the last place in which a witch was burned at the stake, when Mother Lakeland paid that price in 1645 for bewitching her husband to death.

Jane Shore was the mistress of Edward IV (1461–1483). When he died, Richard III accused her of witchcraft, confiscated her property and had her imprisoned in the Tower, but she was soon released for want of evidence. She was later made to walk in penance, clothed in a white sheet and carrying a lighted candle, to St Paul's, where she confessed her sin of being the late king's concubine.

The age-old belief that witches were able to fly on their broomsticks was discounted by an analysis of samples of the pre-flight ointment which they allegedly applied to their bodies. Professor A J Clark established that the ointment contained substantial amounts of aconite (obtained from monkshood or wolfsbane) and belladonna (from the deadly nightshade plant), drugs which affected the heart and caused delirium, and would have given the witches the sensations of levitation and flight.

The last witch executed in Scotland was Janet Horne, in 1722.

A naval 'knot' is a measure of speed, being 1.15mph. Another sort of knot, provided by witches, for a fee of course, allowed sailors to select the strength of wind they wanted and therefore their ship's speed. The witch would provide a short length of rope with three knots tied in it; untying the first knot would guarantee a gentle breeze, two knots, a steady wind, three knots, a gale.

When her husband Lord Glamis died, Lady Jane Douglas married again, but in 1555 she spurned the attentions of William Lyon. Rebuffed, he took revenge by accusing her to the authorities of casting harmful spells on James V of Scotland. She and members of her family were subsequently racked, and Jane herself burned at the stake on Edinburgh's Castle Hill, the flames leaping higher as oil and tar were poured over the branches heaped around her.

In November 1611 a husband and wife, Richard and Anne Jonne, were charged with bewitching to death a horse belonging to a Mr Prentisse. They were also accused of employing, feeding and rewarding several evil spirits, namely 'Jockey', 'Jacke' and 'Will', with the intention of destroying their neighbours' livestock. Richard was hanged, but his wife died before her sentence could be carried out.

In the seventeenth century it was believed that a quill, the long hollow central part of a bird's feather, filled with quicksilver (mercury) and buried beneath the doorway of the house, would keep away witches.

Alice Molland is believed to be the last witch to be hanged, the execution taking place at Exeter in 1684.

One of the exorcisms spoken by priests to drive away evil forces was: 'Deliver this place from all evil spirits, vain imaginations and phantasms, projections and all deceits of the evil one. Bid them harm no one, but to depart to the place appointed them, there to remain for ever. Go forth, thou deceiver, full of all evil and falsehood, the enemy of virtue, the persecutor of the innocent. Give place, thou wicked one; give place, thou evil one; give place to Christ.'

The crime of witchcraft was repealed in 1736, although anyone pretending to practise it could still have charges of being an impostor brought against them.

When Elizabeth I suffered from toothache and insomnia, a Mrs Dier was accused of causing the affliction by conjuring up evil spirits and witchcraft. History does not record her fate; doubtless it was not a pleasant one.

In the reign of Charles II (1660–1685) the law stated that 'witches were to be worried [harassed or tormented] at the stake and then burned.'

In 1883 newspapers in Essex reported the case of a gardener who unearthed the remains of two women. Because the corpses had their arms secured to their legs, a measure supposed to prevent them escaping from their graves, they were identified as witches.

Under the Witchcraft Act of 1735, a spiritualist, Helen Duncan, was accused of being a witch – 209 years later, in 1944. The Act was subsequently repealed and mediums were allowed to continue holding their seances 'as long as it was without intent to deceive'.

During the seventeenth century, one test of whether a woman was a witch or not was to weigh her against the local church Bible; if she weighed less than the heavy tome, the verdict was indisputably one of guilty and the usual outcome was death.

Erichtho, a Roman witch, lived surrounded by the necessary ingredients for her necromantic recipes: eyeballs, tongues, fingers and more intimate body parts taken from corpses in a graveyard. Asked by Sextus, son of Pompey the Great, to predict the future, she obtained a soldier's corpse, which fortunately happened to be complete with tongue, voice box and so forth, and poured into it a concoction of snake skin, mad dog's spit, hyena flesh and noisome herbs. After she had recited various Satanic spells, the soldier's spirit appeared and, reinstating itself in its cadaver, then rose to its feet and delivered the answers to the prophetic questions posed by Erichtho.

In the seventeenth century there was a universally accepted test by which witches could be identifed, that of 'scratching'. The person who alleged they had been bewitched scratched the arm of the suspected witch until blood was drawn; if at that moment the affliction suffered by the victim disappeared, it was absolute proof that the woman scratched was indeed a witch and so would suffer the dire penalties due to her.

Members of Parliament sitting in June 1604 enacted a Statute decreeing that 'any person that shall use any invocation or conjuration of any wicked spirit for any purpose, or shall take up any dead body or part thereof, to be used for sorcery or enchantment, or shall practise witchcraft whereby any person shall be killed, wasted or lamed, shall suffer death as a felon. And further, to the end that all practice of witchcraft shall be abolished, any person that shall take upon him any witchcraft, charm or sorcery to declare where any treasure may be found, or goods lost or stolen, or shall provoke any person to unlawful love, or cause goods or cattle to be destroyed or impaired, shall suffer imprisonment for one whole year, and once in every quarter stand for six hours in the pillory upon market day or at a fair, and confess the error; and if they offend again, then to suffer death.'

To persuade suspected witches to confess their crime, 'wakers' were employed, who would ensure that the women were not allowed to sleep, and would burn their feet and toes with lighted candles until they retracted their denials.

The catalogue of the collection of torture instruments once exhibited in the royal castle of Nuremberg describes an instrument called a 'Witch-Catching Staff'. Under its pointed end, used for prodding, was a hook for catching the witch, making it unnecessary to touch her, for to do so would result in evil spells being cast on the wielder. Further protection was afforded by the words 'Jesus', 'Nazarenum' and 'Ave Maria' inscribed on the staff.

No effort was spared in extracting a confession from Alison Balfour in 1597. Her legs were forced into iron 'boots', which were then heated; her husband was suspended from the rafters by his wrists and heavy weights attached to his ankles; and it was not until her son had been severely whipped and her young daughter had suffered in the thumbscrews that she eventually admitted the charge and paid the inevitable penalty.

Oliver Cromwell was thought by many to be in league with the Devil. This belief was endorsed when, immediately before his death, there was a terrific thunderstorm, which always accompanied the death of a wizard.

Halloween festivities were cancelled in 2004 by the obviously spellbound school authorities in Seattle, Washington, in order to prevent local witches from being offended by the ugly and uncomplimentary effigies paraded around town.

On 28 September 1615 Susan Barker took a skull from a grave in Upminster cemetery and used it to bewitch Mary Stephens so that her body was wasted and mutilated; she later bewitched Edward Ashen and his son so that they languished and died. Found guilty, she was hanged.

The historian Robert Pitcairn, in his book *Ancient Criminal Trials in Scotland, 1488–1624*, published in 1833, reported that seventeenth-century witches were tortured by being stripped of their clothes, then forced to wear hair shirts soaked in vinegar.

AMERICANA ASSORTMENT

The longest living 'tripod' man – born with three legs – was American Frank Lentini, who died in 1966 at the age of 77.

The *American Code of 1650*, published by Silas Andrus in Connecticut in 1830, stipulated that: 'if any person shall committ Burglary by breaking into any dwelling howse, or shall robb any person in the feild or highwayes, such a person so offending shall, for the first offense, bee branded on the forehead with the letter B; if hee shall offend in the same kinde, the second time, hee shall be branded as before, and allso be severely whipped; and if he shall fall into the same offense the third time, hee shall bee put to death as being incorrigible. And if any person shall commit such Burglary, or rob in the feilds or in the howse on the Lord's day, besides the former punishments, hee shall for the first offense have one of his ears cutt off, and for the second offense, in the same kinde, hee shall lose his other ear in the same manner, and if hee falls into the same offense the third time, hee shall be put to death.'

23,438 people were murdered in the USA in 1990.

President Franklin Delano Roosevelt left strict instructions regarding his burial. He was not to be embalmed; he should have just a simple coffin; there should be no hearse but a gun-carriage. Unfortunately the exact opposite of all three requirements took place, since the instructions were not found until after his burial.

On 30 July 1971, the astronauts David Scott (a friend of the author) and Jim Irwin landed on the moon in Apollo 15 and, at the base of a cliff, placed a memorial plaque listing those astronauts and cosmonauts who had lost their lives during the exploration of space.

President Lincoln was elected in 1860, President Kennedy in 1960; both were killed on Fridays, their wives being with them. Both their successors were named Johnson, the former born in 1808, the latter in 1908. Of their assassins, John Wilkes Booth was born in 1839, Lee Harvey Oswald in 1939.

Another oddity: all Presidents elected at twenty-year intervals since 1840 have died in office: first William Henry Harrison; then Lincoln, elected in 1860; Garfield, 1880; McKinley, 1900; Harding, 1920; Roosevelt, 1940, and Kennedy, 1960.

In 1943, 22,572 people were killed in automobile accidents, in the USA, a rate of 62 fatalities per day.

On 24 November 1971 an airline passenger in the USA calling himself Dan Cooper passed a note to the crew threatening to blow the aircraft up unless he was given $200,000. The aircraft landed and, after the money had been handed over, took off again, Cooper having also demanded and been given a parachute. While over a heavily forested area he leapt from the aircraft and, although the 'chute was discovered much later, Cooper and the money were never found.

Forty per cent of all men drafted into the US Army during World War II were found to be physically unfit for active service. Of those stationed in the army of occupation in Germany in 1946, one in four had venereal disease.

Another law in the *1650 Code* stated that 'if any Childe or children above sixteene years old and of sufficient understanding, shall Curse or smite their naturall father or mother, he or they shall bee put to death; unless it can bee sufficiently testified that the parents have been very unchristianly negligent in the education of such children, or so provoke them by extreme and cruell correction that they have beene forced to preserve themselves from death or maiming.'

Identical twins John and Eli Phipps of Virginia set a new record for twins by reaching the age of 108.

In Marksville, Louisiana, on 23 October 1947, a veritable downpour of freshwater fish, up to nine inches in length, fell from the skies, despite the weather being calm and foggy.

The punishment of being exhibited in the pillory was abolished in the USA in 1839, other than in the state of Delaware, where it survived until 1905.

When an American woman was murdered in 2004, her identity was established by the serial numbers stamped on her breast implants.

Some New York shops selling magic tokens and witchcraft artefacts in the 1960s did a roaring trade in ingredients such as bottles of graveyard dust and coins purporting to have been taken from dead men's eyes.

The *Code of 1650* included a seemingly baffling statute, as follows: 'It is ordered that no peage, white or black, bee paid or received, but what is strunge, and in some measure, strunge suitably, and not small and great, uncomely and disorderly mixt, as formerly it hath beene.' Baffled? Well, peage is an uncommon word meaning wampum, the money used by Native Americans, consisting of cylindrical shells strung together, especially white shells, rather than the black or purple ones. So it would appear that money received in the form of shells has to be strung together neatly and in order.

Early in the twentieth century the severed fingers of lynched blacks might be seen in white butcher's shops in Atlanta. Throughout the nation lynchings averaged about five a week, but by 1941 this figure had decreased to four during the year, and in 1945 only one took place.

304,190 Americans lost their lives during World War II; 31,215 were New Yorkers, 26,554 Pennsylvanians and 18,061 were from Illinois. Nevada had the lowest number, 349 men being killed.

Those attending big events love to have a memento of the occasion, so, when Leo Frank was hanged in Georgia in March 1913, the rope was cut into short lengths afterwards and sold to souvenir hunters; those at the back of the queue had to be content with an inch or two of the rope with which his ankles had been bound.

In 1946, the risk of being killed by a faulty New York lift was one in 196,000,000.

Early American rules regarding voting stipulated 'that if any person within these liberties have beene or shall be fyned or whipped for any scandalous offence, hee shall not be admitted, after such tyme, to have any voate in towne or commonwealth, nor to serve on a jury, untill the courte shall manifest their satisfaction.'

In Boston, as late as 1851, black people found on the streets after hours were arrested and imprisoned until the next morning, when they received 39 lashes. The policeman delivering the blows received fifty cents.

An Act of Legislature of 1740 stated: 'In case any person shall wilfully cut out the tongue, put out the eye, or cruelly scald, burn, or deprive any slave of any limb or member, or shall inflict any other cruel punishment *other than* [author's italics] by whipping or beating with a horse-whip, cow-skin, switch or small-stick, or by putting irons on, or confining or imprisoning such slave, every such person shall for every such offence, forfeit the sum of one hundred pounds current money.'

In the nineteenth century an American body-snatcher named 'Old Cunny' provided the Ohio Medical College with corpses for use in dissection lessons – at a price, of course. On one occasion some of the students played tricks on him and in revenge he deliberately sold them the body of a man who had died of smallpox, thereby infecting many of them with the terrible disease.

In New York in the 1650s, an Indian was killed by a cobbler. The murderer was tried and found guilty but, since he was very popular, steps were taken to save him from the scaffold – so an old, bedridden weaver was substituted and hanged in his place.

It was reported in 1947 that the state of Tennessee boasted the biggest man ever known. He was Miles Darden (1798–1857) who, at the age of 47, was 7ft 6in in height and weighed 871lb. He died strangled by the pressure of the fat on his vocal cords, and the side of his house had to be removed to facilitate the removal of his body.

A sign in Connelly's Tavern in Natchez, Mississippi, in 1819, read; 'Fourpence a Night for Bed, Sixpence a Night with Supper, No More than Four to Sleep in a Bed, No Boots to be Worn in Bed, and Organ Grinders to Sleep in the Washhouse'.

In 1828 the National Society of the United States Daughters of 1812 paid for an ornamental archway to be built at Dartmoor prison, England, with the inscription 'To the Glory of God and in loving memory of 218 American sailors and soldiers of the War of 1812 who died here'.

The Vice-President of South Carolina, Henry Laurens, captured at sea by the British in 1780 during the War of American Independence, was accused of plotting to bring Holland into the war on their side and was imprisoned in the Tower of London. Later released, he became a popular dinner guest back home on account of his exploits, and rejoiced in the title of Henry 'Tower' Laurens.

The concrete used to construct the Grand Coulee Dam across the Columbia River in Washington weighed three times as much as the Great Pyramid of Egypt; 23 million tons.

Dalliance was strictly frowned on in seventeenth-century America; for indulging in that sin in 1642, 'John Lobell the Miller, for sinfull dalliance with a little wench of Goodman Halls, was whipped.'

In the 1930s Pennsylvania was great hunting country; two to three hundred bears were killed annually, and many deer, 200,000 of the latter being shot in 1931. Bounties were paid for the extermination of predatory animals, and 8,032 gray foxes and 16,509 weasels were killed in a single season.

In his superb classic *Inside USA*, John Gunther quotes several boasts about Texas: 'it's where you need a mousetrap to catch mosquitos, where a man is so hardboiled that he sleeps in sandpaper sheets; where canaries sing bass, where, if you spill some nails, you will harvest a crop of crowbars; where houseflies carry dogtags for identification, and where, if you shoot at a peccary [a type of pig], it will spit your bullet back, then race it back to you'.

When Alice Pike went shopping in a town in Georgia, USA, she didn't have the exact money for her purchases, so she tendered a one million dollar note instead and waited for her change. Instead the police arrived and she was arrested on a charge of forgery, since notes to that value have never been issued by the Bank of America.

An extract from the ancient records of New-Haven describes how, at a court held in 1643, 'Andrew Lowe, jun., for breaking into Mr. Ling's house, where he brake open a cupboard and took from thence some Strong Water, being Rum, and 6d. in money, and ransackt the House from roome to roome, and left open the doors, for which fact being committed to prison, brake forth and escaped, and still remains horribly obstinate and rebellious against his parents, and incorrigible under all the means that have been used to reclaim him. Whereupon it was ordered that he shall be as severely whipt as the rule will bare, and will work with his father as a prisoner with a lock upon his leg so that he may not escape.'

In 2004 American Dr Morley Engleman opened the door of his house to be faced by homeless vagrant Kevin Graff holding the head of 91-year-old Robert Lees, whom he had just decapitated. The intruder is also believed to have stabbed the doctor to death before being arrested by the Los Angeles police.

Instead of being utilised for anatomical instruction, body-parts belonging to over 800 corpses donated to the University of California in 2003 were instead sold illegally overseas for high prices. They probably cost an arm and a leg.

It is said the winds are so strong in the Texas dustbowl that on one occasion, just as a farmer was arranging with a banker to visit and inspect his farm in order to obtain a loan, the farm blew past the bank.

The American state with the greatest number of earthquakes between 1935 and 1946 was Montana, which had three thousand.

One of the best hotels in Spokane, Washington, in the 1940s was the Davenport. The attention to detail even included ensuring that every coin was washed before being given in change.

When hardy settlers founded the town of Seattle in Washington in the 1860s, there was a desperate shortage of women, so, as reported in the *American Guide Series*, one Asa Mercer travelled to the Atlantic seaboard and returned with a covey of eleven virgins who were willing to marry, sight unseen, the lonely but stalwart pioneers. When they arrived, 'the single men of the town turned out looking like grizzlies in store clothes and their hair slicked down like sea-otters.' In 1866 Mercer brought in 46 more women and proved the virtue of his wares by marrying one of them himself.

The Mormon leader Brigham Young believed in polygamy and had at least 47 children by seventeen wives.

In the 1640s women were actually forced to get married. It was reported in the New-Haven court proceedings for 1643 that

'Margaret Bedforde, being convicted of divers miscarriages [sinful misbehaviour], was ordered to be married to Nicholas Jennings.'

When an earthquake struck Caracas, Venezuela on Good Friday, 29 March 1812, a regiment of soldiers en route to join a religious procession 'was almost wholly swallowed up, a few men only being left alive. Most inhabitants took refuge in the churches, which, being destroyed by the shocks, became their tombs, and in order to avoid the effects of a pestilence, the bodies were piled up in different places and burnt with the timber of the ruins.'

The early English colonists had to protect themselves at all costs, and it was ordained by the members of 'A Courte holden 23rd November 1639, that every one thatt beares Armes [i.e. who can bear arms] shall be compleatly furnished with armes, viz. a muskett, a sword, vandaleers, a rest, a pound of powder, 20 bullets fitted to [of the correct calibre of] their muskett, or 4 pounds of pistol shot or swan shott att least, and be ready to show them in the market place upon Monday the 6th of this moneth, before Captaine Turner and Lieutenant Seeley, under the penalty of 20s fine for every default or absence.'

Following the declaration of war on Japan by the USA in 1942, 125,000 Japanese were rounded up across the country and transferred to relocation centres, where they were held under lock and key until released in January 1945.

An ancient tradition of the Apache tribe forbids married males to speak to or even look at their mothers-in-law.

In 1947 there were more trees in New York – 2,400,000 – than houses, and New Yorkers made 18,200,000 phone calls a day, of which 125,000 were wrong numbers – sorry, caller!

In earlier days in Los Angeles, citizens were forbidden by law to shoot rabbits from streetcars; throw snuff or give it to a child under 16; bath two babies in a single bathtub at the same time; make pickles in any downtown district; or sell snakes on the streets.

Some of the towns set up in California during the Gold Rush days were given such picturesque names as Brandy Gulch, Gouge Eye, Piety Hill, Poker Flat, Swell-Head Diggings and, probably because a certain class of ladies bestowed their favours on the miners for a nugget or two, Petticoat Slide.

'Gumbo' is a type of soil peculiar to South Dakota. It is said that during a drought 'it is so hard that you can see a nickel two miles away, but when it rains, the grass grows so fast that you have to part it to see a cow. When wet it is slippery and sticky; anyone born in gumbo country is long-legged because of the exercise he gets pulling his legs out of it.'

Upon being asked for their impressions of New York, a young English girl replied. 'The steam rising from manholes in the streets, and the fact that so many policemen are so fat!', while a Brazilian commented on 'road signs like those warning motorists "Death is So Permanent!" '

An immense carving of the head of Crazy Horse, proud warrior leader of the Sioux tribe, in the Black Hills of Dakota was started in 1935; 90ft high by 2004, it is planned to be completed by the addition of his torso and arms and his horse's head and mane. The monument will eventually attain a height of 563ft.

There were 4,708 lynchings in the USA between 1882 and 1944; 573 of them occurred in Mississippi, 521 in Georgia and 489 in Texas.

San Francisco in the 1850s was a violent town, more than one thousand murders being committed between 1849 and 1856. A vigilante committee eventually took control and hangings soon became a deterrent; they were carried out in public, accompanied by the tolling of church bells.

The oldest public building in Maine is a gaol built in 1653.

The early English settlers had firm views on intimacy with the opposite sex; under the heading of 'Fornication', their court ordered that 'If any man shall commit fornication with any single woman, they shall bee punnished, either by injoyning to marriage, or fyne, or corporall punnishment, or all, or any of these, as the Courte or magistrates shall appoint, most agreeable to the word of God.'

Nicknames given to the different states in the USA include 'Baby' or 'Valentine' for Arizona, 'Cyclone' and 'Jaywalker' for Kansas, 'Sucker' for Illinois, 'Tar Heel' for North Carolina, 'Coyote' for South Dakota and 'Mud-Waddler' for Mississippi.

The first legalisation of the use of corpses for teaching dissection is believed to have been in the Massachusetts Act of 1784, the corpses to be 'those killed in duels, and those executed for killing in duels'. So win or lose, you got the chop.

In 1946 Americans consumed 1,115 million quarts of ice-cream and 660 million doughnuts (burp!).

The number of rural homes without either toilet or privy in the USA in 1940 was 695,662; the states suffering most inconvenience were North Carolina, with 74,482; Mississippi, 65,886; Tennessee, 56,946; Texas, 46,855; and Georgia and South

Carolina, both lacking 41,924 loos. By contrast, all but 48 homes in the state of Rhode Island were flushed with success.

San Diego, California, boasts the 'shortest thermometer' in the country, with an average summer temperature of 68 degrees and a winter temperature of 55.

The state of Oregon was ruled jointly by America and Great Britain for 28 years.

The longest and straightest street in the world is believed to be O Street, part of US Highway 34 in Nebraska; it measures 69 miles without a bend.

The current controversy concerning the right of a householder to defend himself against burglars never arose in the American colony of the 1600s, for a law was passed that 'if any person in the just and necessary defence of his life, or the life of any other, shall kill any person attempting to rob or murther in the feilds or higheway, or to breake into any dwelling howse, if hee conceive hee cannot with safety of his owne person, otherwise take the ffellon, or assailant and bring him to tryall, hee shall be houlden blameless.'

Women found guilty of adultery in the early Puritan days had to have a letter 'A' sewn on their dresses as a badge of shame.

SOME ODD FACTS

Some nineteenth-century coffins were made of lead and, unless they were watched and 'tapped' (vented) to allow the mephitic vapour to escape, tended to burst. An undertaker stated: 'I was once called out at midnight by some people who were in great alarm, and who claimed that the coffin had burst in the night, with a report like the sound of a cannon being fired. I found that it had been a death from dropsy, very rapid decomposition had occurred, and the lead was forced up. I have heard of similar cases from other undertakers.'

A veritable rabbit warren of tunnels and passages, the remains of old quarries from which was extracted the limestone used in building the city, exists beneath the street of Paris; many are as yet unexplored.

Sightings of UFOs are reported from many countries across the world; in Spanish they are *objectos volantes no identificados*; in Chinese, *fei tieh*; in Japanese, *sora tobu emban*; in Arabic, *sohhoun taa'ira*; in Italian, *ojetti volanti non identificati*, and in the Pacific Islands, *akuatele*.

Those traversing the Rotherhithe Tunnel in London are advised not to linger; between its roof and the bed of the Thames are only seven feet of sand!

When, in 2004, a woman's husband died, she still wanted to keep him close at hand, so she had his ashes refined into carbon and formed into a diamond, which she had set in a ring, and wore.

It was reported in detail in the journal *La Domenica del Corriere* of 29 December 1946 that an elderly Sicilian peasant, Concetto Buonsignore, had suddenly started to babble. The gibberish was identified by Palermo professors as a Greek dialect dating back to 405 BC. After five days he reverted to his normal Italian.

Roman ladies vied with each other over who had the most grotesque or misshapen dwarf in her household as a personal servant.

Matthew Clydesdale was sentenced to be hanged on 4 November 1818 and then to be dissected at Glasgow University. When the corpse was taken there, it was given a 'galvanic shock', whereupon 'it stood up and faced the astonished students!' Professor Jeffrey immediately picked up a lancet and plunged it into the jugular vein, causing the cadaver 'to collapse like a slaughtered ox'! No further orders for dissection were given by the Glasgow court.

The name 'hearse' is derived from a word in Old French for 'harrow', since in earlier times one was suspended above the coffin and used as a chandelier, with candles stuck on the spikes.

Fearing being buried while still alive, in 1895 a man insisted that when he died he should be interred in his garden with a switch in his hand connected to an alarm in the house. A good idea, although if one's house is sold later and the new owner disturbs the ground by digging, then investigates the noise . . .

A walking stick and a ghost were offered for sale on the internet in 2004, advertised by an American woman whose six-year-old son thought their house was haunted by his grandfather, the owner of the walking stick. Offers of £40 were received.

The classification of fingerprints for identification purposes was developed by Sir Edward Henry and adopted by the UK in 1902 and the USA in 1903/4.

In March 1610 John Davies and Thomas Carter were found guilty of coining, manufacturing eight King James shillings and six Elizabeth sixpences from base metal. Both were 'drawn to the place of execution and hanged'.

To have a fear of flowers is Anthophobia; of darkness, Nyctophobia; of dead bodies, Necrophobia; of being buried alive, Taphephobia; of death, Thanatophobia.

The marble on the front of the crypt of Marilyn Monroe in Los Angeles is covered with lipstick kisses pressed there by admiring fans.

During the French Revolution men had wax tablets made, incorporating the image of the guillotine, with which to seal their letters.

The word 'clairvoyance' is derived from the French and literally means 'clear seeing'.

In eighteenth-century France, offenders condemned to be branded had their heads shaved, to prevent them covering their faces with their hair when appearing on the scaffold to receive their punishment.

A 'cod-piece' is a bag covering the male 'privities'; a 'merkin' is a small wig to cover the female equivalent.

The first communication using the electric telegraph occurred in 1830. Because of the slow reactions of the man at the other end, the first ever message was 'Fast asleep by the fire!'

The famous French forensic scientist Edmond Locard stated that he could identify, with an accuracy of 92%, the dust trapped in the wax in the ears of a suspect. So minute coffee grains in the ears of a man suspected of a coffee-shop murder would have been grounds for arrest!

A nineteenth-century Irish girl, Annie Jackson, grew twisted horns from her elbows, arms and forehead. The details were reported in the book *Anomalies and Curiosities of Medicine*, published in 1896.

John Rocque brought out one of the earliest maps of London in 1747. It consisted of 24 sheets covering an area of 6½ft by 13ft. Totally unopenable in a car.

The word 'Assize', as in Assize Court, is from the Latin *adsideo*, meaning 'I sit by, attend' and was originally applied to an assembly of knights who sat in judgement.

London Bridge, built in 1176, was London's first stone built crossing of the Thames, and remained in place for five centuries; a successor, designed by Rennie, lasted only 135 years before being transported to Florida as a tourist attraction.

The preserved corpse of Lenin, the founder of the Soviet Union, who died in 1924, rests in a glass cabinet in Moscow. The tomb is inspected weekly to check the temperature and humidity and, if necessary, to retouch the cadaver's face and hands with rouge and powder.

Sentenced to be beheaded, Lord William Russell mounted the scaffold on 29 December 1681, to be loudly jeered at by the immense crowd of spectators. When he appealed to the officials present, Sheriff Bethel, with brutal humour, replied, 'Sir, we have orders to stop nobody's breath but yours!'

Bingo originated in Italy early in the sixteenth century, when it was known as *Lo Giuoco del Lotto d'italia.*

The 34-carat 'Napoleon' diamond was bought by Napoleon Bonaparte in the 1790s for the immense sum of £8,000, and worn by him mounted in the hilt of his sword.

After some seven attempts had been made on Queen Victoria's life, a parasol lined with chain-mail was made for her protection, but proved too heavy to be of use.

Although dyslexic, the world-famous Danish author Hans Christian Andersen refused to be handicapped by his impaired ability to read, and spoke his stories out loud so that his secretary could write them down for him.

In 1564 John Summerfield, aged three, was married to Jane Brerton, aged two. The groom was carried in his uncle's arms to the altar and held 'while the words of matrimony were in speaking'. Many such marriages were later annulled.

When sentenced to death by the guillotine, M. Moyse, found guilty of murdering his own son, said indignantly, 'What, would you execute the father of a family?!'

A Temple of Health was opened in London in 1779 by James Graham, containing a 'celestial bed', the hire of which was 'guaranteed to result in conception by its occupants.' An article in the

British Medical Journal in 1911 described it as 'a sumptuous bed in brocaded damask, supported by four crystal pillars of spiral shape festooned with garlands of flowers in gilded metal; and for a fee of fifty guineas [£52.50] Dr. Graham offers couples, old and young, the means of getting offspring. While in the bed one hears four organs playing, which carry the happy couple into the arms of Morpheus. For nearly an hour that the concert lasts, one sees streams of light, which play especially over the pillows. When the time for getting up has come, the magician comes to feel the pulse of the faithful, gives them breakfast, and sends them away full of hope, not forgetting to recommend them to send him other clients.' One of Graham's assistants was a young girl, Emma Lyon, who later became Lady Hamilton, an intimate friend of Lord Nelson.

During the reign of Henry II (1154–1189), the Lord Chancellor, when on royal tour with his master, received 5s a day, a simnel (a piece of bread or cake), a measure of household wine, one large wax candle and forty pieces of small candle. However, if he dined at home he received only 3s 6d a day.

It wasn't only felons who transgressed the law; in 1619 Thomas Cooper, keeper of Colchester Gaol, was remanded to a Grand Jury for keeping an unauthorised alehouse in the gaol and allowing prisoners and 'evil disposed' outsiders to drink inordinately.

Nearly 1,800 families lost their homes when London's Marylebone Station was constructed in 1898.

During World War II the Domesday Book and other historic documents normally held by the Public Record Office were stored for safety in Shepton Mallet Gaol in Somerset.

For bigamously marrying Mary Samms in 1622 when his wife also named Mary was still alive, William Foster was hanged.

A clear case of Nimbyism (Not In My Back Yard) occurred in Brigg, Lincolnshire, in 1827, when a local chimney-sweep was sentenced to be executed and hanged in chains. But the inhabitants petitioned against the gibbetting because it was too near town, so that part of the sentence was remitted.

When the Royal Courts of Justice were built in the Strand in 1886, over four thousand people were moved out of their homes, which were then demolished. In the building are more than two and a half miles of corridors. The great stone pillars on the ground floor are hollow and contain a spiral stairway leading to upper floors.

In the sixteenth century a woman who had been found guilty of speaking lies and uttering false rumours was taken by the hangman to Cheapside, near St Paul's Cathedral, and nailed by her ears to the pillory there.

A young Norfolk lady bought the coffin of her choice in 2004 and occasionally lies in it to get used to the idea.

The diesel engine was invented by Rudolph Diesel, a German engineer born in Paris in 1858. Mystery surrounds his death, for he vanished from an English Channel steamer in September 1913. Presumed lost overboard, his body was never found.

In ancient Egypt adultery was classed as a heinous crime. Guilty men were punished with mutilation, and a woman who committed adultery had her nose cut off.

William Poole, George Portingalle, Elizabeth Johnson and Honor Johnson were found guilty of disguising themselves as 'Egyptians' (gypsies) and impersonating them for a month prior to 26 June 1608 for the purpose of begging. All four were hanged, after the Jury of Matrons had confirmed that neither woman was pregnant.

In the 1700s there was a Turkish bath in Covent Garden where ladies were invited to indulge in 'Sweating, Bathing and Cupping'. The last of these involved a heated cup being applied to the skin; the blister it caused was then punctured to draw off contaminated blood.

Winners of battles celebrate by taking mementos of their dead enemies. North American Indians used to remove their foes' scalps, African tribesmen their enemy's heads. Civilised countries refrained from such barbaric practices; instead they hanged the enemies of society, smeared plaster over their faces, made casts, and created death-masks from the moulds. One in the author's possession is of bronze, the eyes closed, the facial features perfectly delineated, but, alas, his identity is unknown.

When, in 1767, the robber Patrick Redmond was hanged, a confederate bribed the hangman to cut him down before the regulation hour had elapsed, so after 29 minutes the 'corpse' was rushed to a neighbouring house where, after massage and bloodletting, the victim revived so completely that he was able to attend the local theatre in Cork. There, mounting the stage to tumultuous applause, he gave credit to his ally, 'whereup the audience took up a genteel collection for him'.

A Malaysian man who never gives up hope has just returned to his first wife – after having married 51 others!

In the early eighteenth century Scottish judges sentenced the guilty to be executed between two and four o'clock in the afternoon. One condemned man, John Young, concluded that if he could delay being escorted to the scaffold until after four o'clock, he could go free! Accordingly he barricaded the cell door, but those who came to collect him were determined that the law should run its course, and so workmen took up part of the floor immediately above his cell, and six warders then dropped down and seized him. His protests that it was then six o'clock were abruptly terminated as the drop trap-doors opened.

An overhaul of outdated laws in Queensland, Australia, included those which made it illegal to wear slippers in the street, to be in a stable carrying a dark lantern or to tell fortunes in a flea market.

There's nothing new about the illegality of carrying an edged weapon in cities. Six hundred years ago a law decreed that anyone simply drawing a sword from its scabbard should be fined ten shillings or spend two weeks in gaol. Injuring anyone with the weapon carried a fine of £1 – a substantial sum in those days – or forty days imprisonment.

The renowned novelist William Makepeace Thackeray was among the crowd of spectators at a public execution in 1840. He afterwards described the windows surrounding the execution site as 'full of quiet family parties of honest tradesmen, sipping tea with calm, and moustached dandies squirting the throng below with brandy and water'.

The word 'beads' comes from the Anglo-Saxon *biddan,* meaning 'to pray', *bed* being a prayer. So the word is derived from the practice of fingering beads one by one while saying prayers.

In 2004 a German therapist inserted the requisite number of acupuncture needles into his patient, busied himself elsewhere and eventually locked up and went home. It was only hours later that he remembered and returned to the surgery, where he found his patient unharmed – though somewhat needled.

Robbery was rife in the seventeenth century. It was reported that 'Sir Henry Goodyere had his room broken into at Court and £120 stolen; Sir Adolphus Carew lost £50 and three suits of apparel, and at the same time my Lady Dorothy Hastings, who lay in the room above him, was spoiled of all that God ever sent her, save that which she had on her back and her belly.'

Germans shopping around in 2004 for cheap funerals for deceased relatives might well take advantage of an offer by a firm of undertakers who will have the body cremated and buried in the Czech Republic for half the German price.

Until about the middle of the nineteenth century, Scottish policemen performed a dual role; as well as having to watch out for lawbreakers while on the early morning shift, they also had to ring a hand-bell to remind residents to throw their rubbish into the streets, ready for the refuse collectors to sweep it up and take it to the city dump. The possibility that the sound of the bell would warn villains of the approach of the Law was obviously overlooked.

MORE ODD FACTS

South African David Masenta shot and killed his pregnant fiancée during a quarrel, then committed suicide, but because their families believed that they would have been happy when married, both corpses were dressed in their wedding outfits and the ceremony was performed by their local priest. Their burials took place shortly afterwards.

That a time warp of some kind operates in the Bermuda Triangle on the east coast of America is evidenced by a case in which a Boeing 727 in that area disappeared from ground radar screens for ten minutes. On landing, all timepieces on board, both passengers' watches and those on the aircraft's instrument panels, were found to have lost ten minutes.

Sir Benjamin Rudyard wrote: 'France is a good country to ride through, Italy a good country to look upon, Spain a good country to understand, but England a good country to live in.'

The *Gentleman's Magazine* of September 1762 reported that during a church service, when the wedding banns were read out, a woman stood up and loudly declared that she had been married to the would-be groom for fourteen years – and had borne him seven children.

When Eva Coo was being tried for murder in New York in 1935, the judge tried to put the jury at ease by saying, 'Do not feel we are locking you up; enjoy yourselves, laugh and chat, get plenty of exercise. You are good sports and good citizens, and I appreciate what you are doing.'

Until the practice was abolished in Germany in 1536, an accused person would be brought into court even if he or she had died. Since the corpse was not in full possession of its faculties (!), a lawyer would present a defence on its behalf. Obviously, justice had to be seen to be done.

In Victorian times the Pool of London was always full of shipping, requiring Tower Bridge to open several times a day. Should any horses pulling vehicles across the bridge fall or become otherwise incapacitated, reserve horses from stables on the bridge were immediately brought out and hitched up.

Over the centuries there has always been a ready market for gruesome relics of executions, whether as souvenirs or charms or for use in medicines. Short lengths of the ropes used to hang notorious criminals brought high prices, as did coffin nails, and even segments of the victim's skin. The author has in his possession a small Scottish guide book whose front and back covers are thin sheets of wood inscribed 'Made from the wood of the Old Gallows Tree at Doune Castle'.

A forerunner of the London taxi was the sedan chair, a cubicle with a seat in it, transported by two men, one at the front, the other at the back, who gripped the poles fixed to each side and ran with it. The chairs were introduced into England in 1634 by Sir Sanders Duncombe, who named them after seeing them in Sedan. Daniel Defoe, writing in 1702, commented that 'We are carried to the coffee-houses in 'chairs' which are here very cheap, a guinea (£1 1s) a week or a shilling an hour.' Aristocrats had their own sedan chairs, carried by servants wearing the family livery. The Exchequer records include a bill for a sedan chair made for Charles II's mistress, Nell Gwynne costing £34 11s, and another for chair hire amounting to £1 11s 6d.

Sir Roger Casement was sentenced to death for treason during World War I. When visited in his room in the Tower of London by the officer commanding the troops there, Sir Roger said that the sentry guarding him knew a lot about the history of the Tower. 'For instance,' he said, 'he told me that no prisoner who had occupied my cell had ever succeeded in escaping the gallows,' adding, with a smile, 'and from what my defence council told me this morning, I don't think I'm going to prove an exception to the rule!' He was duly hanged in Pentonville Prison on 3 August 1916.

Owing to a yellowish pigment in the whites of his eyes, Napoleon possessed a particularly hypnotic and awesome stare.

The bill for executing Robert Scott in Berwickshire in 1823 included 'cutting Scott's hair, 2d; for shaving him eleven times, 1s 10d; to a joiner for affixing a chair into the cart to take him to the scaffold, 3s 6d; for a cheese to men at the scaffold, 6d; for a lanthorn for escorting the corpse to Edinburgh for dissection, 3d; to refreshment at Carfrae Mill en route for men and horse, 3s 6d; for victuals for eleven men guarding scaffold, £1 6s 10d.'

In 2004 a schoolboy in Japan was punished for dozing off by being ordered to write a hundred lines – in his own blood. The teacher even gave him a knife with which to slit his finger.

Twenty-seven road or rail bridges cross the 69 miles between the mouth of the River Thames and Teddington.

The saying 'a man of straw' meaning one whose opinions can be swayed either way, originates from the early nineteenth-century practice whereby professional perjurers would walk around the courts at Westminster with straws in their shoes to advertise that they could be hired to give favourable evidence in a court case.

Among the anatomical curiosities held in the Royal College of Surgeons is a 'two-headed' skull, that of a nineteenth-century child to whose head is attached a smaller integral head complete with eyes, nose and mouth.

When, in 1826, the clergyman present on the Bench suddenly collapsed and died while reciting the session's opening prayers, the judge, Lord Deas (known in criminal circles as Lord Death), after the body had been removed from his side, expressed his sorrow, said that the circumstances were painful and added, 'Bring another minister!'

The large entrance doors in ancient castles usually have small, very narrow doors, known as 'posterns' or 'wicket gates', set in them, through which only one person at a time can enter; having to bend one's head and step over the high 'step' makes it impossible for an attacker to avoid a blow delivered by a defender.

In Victorian society, no gentleman whose breath or clothes might possibly smell of tobacco should be in the company of ladies, nor should he have eaten onions during the past few hours.

The Edwardians considered it unacceptably discourteous to stand or sit with feet wide apart, to contradict one's companions or to stand with hands on hips.

There were many outlandish museums in the eighteenth century. John Salter's Coffee House in Cheyne Walk, Chelsea, displayed not only what were allegedly the Queen of Sheba's fan, William the Conqueror's sword and the shirts worn by Robinson Crusoe and his man Friday, but an item of headgear described as 'Pontius Pilate's Wife's Chambermaid's Sister's Hat'!

To cure a cyst on a child's face, the *Gentleman's Magazine* of April 1758 recommended that the infant be taken to the scaffold on Hanging Day and the hangman be persuaded to stroke the blemish nine times with the deceased felon's hand.

For years after Tower Bridge had been built, any occasion when it was under repair had to be indicated to those in charge of river craft by a bundle of hay suspended from it by day, and a lantern by night.

Following a number of attacks on unsuspecting females in Peterborough in August 1900, police patrolled the area wearing plain clothes 'and noiseless boots'.

Transport authorities in Japan have given a railway halt on the island of Shikoku the name 'Sorry'; nearby is a railway station named 'Thank you'. One wonders if the terminus further along the line is called 'Don't mention it'.

Footpad John Hartley assaulted and robbed a poor tailor in 1722 and was sentenced to death, but six young women, dressed in white, went to St James' Palace and presented a petition to George I, in which Hartley promised that if he were pardoned, the girls would cast lots as to which one should be his wife. But His Majesty replied that 'he thought hanging would be better for him than marriage' – so hanged he was.

Ladies in the 1790s were advised to darken their tresses by using a black lead brush, as on a grate, 'although it does come off on the linen'.

Queensland residents may have been forbidden to wear slippers outdoors, but in Carmel, California, the wearing of high-heeled shoes is illegal, and if, in flouting the law, one trips over a broken paving stone, no compensation is forthcoming.

Traffic jams are hardly new. On one July day in 1811 traffic enumerators stationed at the City end of London Bridge logged 2,925 drays (open-backed lorries), 1,240 coaches, 769 wagons, 485 gigs (two-wheeled carriages drawn by a single horse), 764 horses and riders and 89,640 pedestrians.

In 1664 a London publisher, William Lee, wrote a little book entitled *The Worth of a Penny*. Among the entries are:

'For a Penny you may buy a fair cucumber, but not a Breast of Mutton, unless it be maggotty.'

'For a Penny a drunkard may be guarded to his lodging, if the evening be dark.'

'For a Penny a chambermaid may buy as much red ochre as will last for seven years, for the painting of her cheeks.'

'At the Apothecaries, you may buy a pennyworth of Lozenges for a Cold, a Diachilon plaster for a boil, Paracelsus, Oil of Roses or Oil of St John's Wort, for a sprain, Jallop to give a purge, Mithridate to make you sweat if infected, and Diascordium Diacodium if you cannot sleep.'

Edward Leigh MA advised those considering travelling abroad in the seventeenth century: to be aged over eighteen; to be able to speak Latin; to be 'grounded in the true religion, lest he be seduced and perverted'; to carry maps of every country he visits, and 'Before his voyage he should make his peace with GOD, receive the Lord's Supper, satisfy his creditors if he be in debt, pray earnestly to GOD to keep him from danger, and should make his last will and order all his affairs, since many that go far abroad, return not home.'

More travel advice: Johnson, in his *Relation of the Many Famous Kingdoms*, warned tourists to 'take heed of the pride of Spain, the poison of Italy, the treason of France, and the drink of Flanders.'

Shortly before Sir Walter Raleigh was executed on 29 October 1618, his barber, Peter, said, 'Sir, we have not curled your hair this morning.' To which Sir Walter replied, 'Let them comb it as shall have it!'

Patent no. 887 of 1767 was for a machine which would preserve men and women 'by fumigating every part of the body, even the most intimate male parts, as if in a steam bath, or baking it in dry heat.'

Mr Hemmings of Trinity College, Cambridge, gave a sermon in St Paul's in April 1603, in which he said that 'if a man would marry, it were a thousand to one but he should light upon a bad woman, there were so many of them; and if he should chance to find a good one, yet he were not sure to hold her so, for women are like a bowl full of snakes amongst which there is one eel, and a thousand to one, if a man happen upon the eel, and if he get it with his hand, all he has gotten is a wet eel by the tail.'

Cromwell's Long Parliament passed a law 'By which all Stage Plays are absolutely forbidden; the stages, seats, galleries etc. to be pulled down. All players, if convicted of acting, to be punished as Rogues, the money received by them to go to the poor of the parish, and every spectator to pay five shillings, also to go to the poor.'

The fashion in the nineteenth century was to leave visiting cards at friends' houses, without knocking at the door. A code was used: simply to say hello, or good wishes, the left-hand upper corner would be bent down; to convey a message of sympathy, the left-hand lower corner similarly bent, and to inform the resident that one was going away for a long time, the right-hand end of the card would receive similar treatment.

To eighteenth-century travellers in the north of England, wooden frames dotting the fields were a common sight; over them would be stretched manufactured articles of wool, so that they could dry out without shrinkage. The frames were known as tenters, and the pieces were held taut by hooks. Hence being 'on tenterhooks' – under strain.

German autobahn traffic came to a dead stop in 2003 when a hearse swerved violently, the rear doors opened and the coffin skidded across the carriageway.

Archibald Campbell, ninth Earl of Argyll, supported the abortive Monmouth Rebellion of 1685 and was sentenced to be beheaded by the guillotine-like Scottish Maiden. On the scaffold he bowed his neck beneath its pendant blade, commenting wryly that 'it was the sweetest maiden he'd ever kissed!'

In 1709 Dick Hughes was on the way to the scaffold when he happened to meet his wife, who asked him who had to provide the rope with which he was to be hanged, she or the sheriff. He replied that it was the official's responsibility. Mrs Hughes said with regret that she'd already bought one, to which hubby replied that it need not be wasted, because she'd probably marry again. His wife agreed, adding, 'If I have the same luck in choosing a husband, so it may!'

During the South African Boer War a battle took place in which many soldiers were killed. Years later investigations established the reason for the flourishing peach orchard which had grown on the site: prior to the battle, many of the men had eaten peaches from nearby trees, and their corpses, buried there, nurtured the seeds, thus producing excellent crops of peaches decades later.

When Mrs Manning was hanged in 1849 she was dressed completely in black. A *Punch* cartoon of the day showed one wax figure in Mme Tussaud's Museum exclaiming to another, 'I've a nice black satin dress – I've only worn it once!'

One cannot but admire the panache of the French aristocrat who, when offered a glass of rum to fortify him before being taken to the guillotine, waved it away with the comment 'No thanks – I lose all sense of direction when I'm drunk!'

While talking to a colleague on the telephone, the Cuban ambassador to the United Nations paused on hearing a hastily smothered cough; realising the line was bugged, he said sarcastically, 'I recommend some cough medicine,' whereupon the eavesdropper replied, 'Thank you very much!'

Anton Mesmer (1734–1815) believed that he could heal people suffering from hysteria with 'animal magnetism'. To 'mesmerise' people, he used a large tub partially filled with water to which had been added iron filings and powdered glass. From sealed bottles of 'magnetised' water, cords were attached round the waists of his patients, who sat round the tub. Other cords had small pieces of iron rod at their extremities, which the patients pressed against the 'diseased' parts of their bodies, the curative effect being enhanced by the good doctor pointing his wand at it. Fashionable society flocked to his sessions, but in 1785 a learned commission reported unfavourably on his methods and he died in obscurity in Switzerland.

The priest of an Italian town was naturally pleased when, in 2004, he received grateful thanks from the local parishioners whose cars he blessed; but doubtless he exclaimed rather more than just 'Good heavens!' when, only hours later, one of them collided with his vehicle.

In the 1840s a Dr Alphonse Teste would hypnotise a volunteer, then 'transfer' that person's 'sensitivity' to a glass of magnetised water; when he pushed a pin into the water, the volunteer would feel the pain, but none when he or she were pricked. He could also induce the volunteer to taste the water and swear that it was lemonade or wine.

Few mediaeval churches and chapels had pews; members of the congregation either stood or knelt before the Lord while worshipping. However, for the benefit of the aged or infirm, benches were positioned around the sides, which gave rise to the saying 'The weakest go to the wall'.

The Domesday Book, an inventory of England compiled by order of its new ruler, William the Conqueror, in 1086, estimated the population at just over one million. Even five hundred years later, it had increased only sixfold – fewer than the number of those living in London today.

Claiming that washing 'prevented a free and constant exhalation from the skin', Thomas Walker ceased to perform his ablutions in 1835. The comments of his wife and close companions were not recorded.

It was a tradition in some parts of the country for relatives of a dead woman to tie her big toes together 'in order to preserve her modesty'.

Necromancy is a method by which the future can be foretold by using dead bodies. Briefly, the practitioners, clad in shrouds stolen from a corpse, gather round a grave at night and burn herbs such as hemlock, mandrake and henbane. They then open the earth to reveal the coffin. The lid is removed, the sorcerer touches the cadaver three times, repeats the secret formula and orders it to rise. It does so, and, in a hollow voice, answers any prophetic questions asked of it, before being returned to its coffin.

Mary Hamilton adopted the guise of a man, keeping her surname but being variously known as George, Charles or William. In 1746, as a man, she married no fewer than fourteen times. The last bride suspected nothing during the first three months of the marriage until she discussed 'certain circumstances' with a married couple who lived nearby. As a result, Mary was arrested and the judge sentenced 'he, she, whichever he or she may be' not only to six months imprisonment, but also to be whipped through the towns of Taunton, Glastonbury, Wells and Shipton Mallet.

In 2004 Dutch women complained to the police that while sunbathing in the city parks they felt their toes being licked by a man, who then ran away. The offender was captured but released; footpads would have been prosecuted, but toe-tasting wasn't a crime.

A devout believer in Spiritualism, the Estonian Baron Ludwig de Guldenstubbe wrote a book published in Paris in 1857 describing how, wishing to contact some of the notable personalities of the past, he left writing paper by their statues in the famous cathedrals and churches throughout Paris. To his amazement he found, on his return, that messages had been roughly scrawled on the paper. That if could have been the mischievous work of a hoaxer was out of the question for, he averred, the brief notes were written in the native language of the statues; the few words left by Roman dignitaries were in Latin, others in Greek, and where the deceased had been English, so were the words.

Things are looking up! In 2003 scientists calculated that there were about 70 sextillion stars visible in the night skies; that's 7 followed by 22 zeros.

During World War II, when iron and similar metals were in desperately short supply, a brilliant inventor, Geoffrey Pyke (1894–1948), proposed that the shortage of warships could be rectified by the manufacture of immensely long 'frozen battleships/aircraft carriers' made from a mixture of ice and wood pulp, which would be virtually indestructible by torpedoes or bombs. Feasibility studies of such vessels were carried out but were cancelled when, in June 1944, D-Day took place.

When Lord Lovat, a leader of the Jacobite Rebellion of 1745, was climbing the steps of the Tower Hill scaffold assisted by his two yeoman warders, he looked at the large crowd assembled to watch him being beheaded. 'God save us!' he exclaimed, 'Why should there be such a commotion about taking an old grey head off that cannot get up a few steps without three bodies to support it?!'

WHOSE ZOO

Apollo the lion escaped from a circus in New York in 2004 and, since there was no zebra crossing nearby, strolled across the Parkway, causing a considerable traffic disruption, until police and its trainer lured it back into captivity.

As an amulet to guarantee good fortune, some South Americans always carry in their pocket the tip of a puma's tongue.

A fishy story, but a true one, concerns the capture in Antarctica of a giant squid with eyes as big as soup plates and eight arms lined with sharp hooks. Weighing in at 150kg, it proved a far from easy catch for the fishermen who discovered it in their nets.

Sharks have a life-span of about a hundred years, and almost never sleep.

Bear-baiting in England was not made illegal until 1835.

On 5 August 1604 a lioness in the Tower Menagerie gave birth to a cub. It was reported in *Court News* that 'the event so greatly entertained the King [James I]'s mind that he gave orders to the Lieutenant of the Tower to have special care for the feeding and warm keeping of it, and that it should not be disturbed by the opening of the Menagerie to the public.' As soon as it was born, its mother carried it in her mouth from place to place, but the keeper took it from her – 'however whether by the dam's bruising of it, or by some other accident, it is dead. It is now bowelled and embalmed, and is to be presented to the King.'

Wolves were always a threat to the early American settlers, so the *Code of 1650* decreed that 'Whereas great loss and dammage doth befall this Commonwealth by reason of wolves, which destroy great numbers of our cattle, it is ordered by this Courte that any person, either English or Indian, that shall kill any wolfe or wolves, within ten myles of any plantation within this jurissdiction, shall have for every wolfe by him or them so killed, ten shillings paid out of the Treasurye of the country; and allso, bring a certificate from the constable of that Place, unto the Treasurer.'

The first commercially cloned cat was created in the USA in 2004 at a cost of £26,000.

The cost of feeding each member of the crew of a warship on anti-drug patrols in the Caribbean is £2.80 a day, but the rations for Casper, the ship's sniffer dog, cost £3: an amount not to be sniffed at.

A court hearing was held in 1949 in which a woman who had been kicked by a horse while it was being led at a racecourse sued the trainer. To demonstrate what happened, the stuffed head of a horse, a display model borrowed from a nearby harness shop, was led around the courtroom by an usher, convincing the jury and resulting in the woman losing the case.

In 2004, wasps in Birmingham were getting high on the fermented fruit of a pear tree and drunkenly attacking local residents; entomological sobriety was restored when the tree was felled.

Horse-shoes bring good luck, but the ones with four nails on one side and three on the other bring by far the best results.

The legend of Dick Whittington and his cat could well be mythical and based on an engraved portrait, made by Reginald Elstrack in the 1590s, in which Dick was originally shown standing with his hand resting on a skull; apparently people would not buy prints of this, so the skull was replaced by a cat, and sales soared.

When, in 2004, Malaysian police investigated women's complaints about the length of time their husbands were spending at a pigsty in their town, they found that it was a brothel.

In order to seize men for naval service, one press gang placed a turkey on top of the Monument in London, then forcibly kidnapped many of the men who stood there open-mouthed looking up at the bird.

In 2004 police raided a flat in a block in Edinburgh and found a 17lb, 4ft alligator splashing in the occupant's bath; he had bought it as a pet. A loofah would have been much more useful.

The first zoo in England, the Royal Menagerie, was situated at the Tower of London; the human residents within the walls had to endure constant roaring and howling – to say nothing of the appalling smells.

The ill-luck caused by walking under a ladder can be neutralised by remaining silent until a four-legged animal is seen.

Introduced into Italy in 1950 for the benefit of hunters, wild boars, which can weigh up to four hundred pounds, are now proving a problem, not only by causing serious damage in gardens, vineyards and Christmas tree plantations but by threatening to maim or kill human beings, of whom they have little fear.

A man-eating lion which attacked villagers in Tanzania, devouring more than thirty of them during a two-year reign of terror, was finally captured and killed in 2004. A veterinary post-mortem revealed that it had what must have been an excruciating abscess under one of its teeth; evidently it had found that human flesh didn't need as much chewing as its normal diet.

Melissa Sweeney, a resident of Texas, left two horses in a field for four months without feeding them. Found guilty of neglecting the animals, she was sentenced to 30 days in gaol, for the first three days of which her meals were to consist of just bread and water.

From the fourteenth to the eighteenth century, cock-fighting was a major sport in big English cities, and London had many cock-pits. Orchestra 'pits' in theatres may derive their name from the fact that early cock-fights took place in such venues.

In the Ozark Mountains of the USA, girls would attract men by hiding the beard of a wild turkey about their persons, while those who lived in Texas were said to carry a horned toad with them (exactly where is not divulged).

In the Middle East during World War II it was necessary to prevent condensation that had mixed with the petrol from entering the fuel tanks of aircraft while they were being refuelled; this was achieved by pouring the petrol through a filter of chamois leather, which allowed petrol to pass through, but not water.

In a book published in 1834, the author Thomas Keightley reports that 'Cats, as we know them, fetched a high price in America when it was first colonised by the Spaniards. Two cats, we are told, were exported on speculation to Cuyaba, where there was a plague of rats, and they were sold for a pound of gold. Their first kittens fetched each thirty pieces of eight, the next generation not more than twenty, and the price gradually fell as the colony became stocked with them.'

An elderly woman died a hideous death by being eaten by a great white shark while swimming near Cape Town in 2004.

Ancient recipes for love-potions included bats' blood, baked doves and powdered mice-feet.

In the records of the New-Haven court, USA, for the year of 1639, were items such as 'Ellice, Mr. Eaton's boy, was whipped for stealing a sow and a goate from his master and selling them', and another ordering that 'Mr. Wilkes shall pay 5 bushells and a halfe of Indian corne to Thomas Buckingham, for corne destroyed by Mr. Wilks' hogs.'

At 99 Holborn Hill, London, in the 1750s, a Mr Gough had a menagerie, where for a shilling visitors could see an ostrich; Gough also bought and sold 'Birds and Beasts'.

In order to protect his vegetables from thieves, a German allotment holder erected an electric fence around the plot, only to be fined £700 when a neighbour's dachshund was electrocuted by it. No doubt he paid with a cheque drawn on his current account.

Poisonous grotesque-looking cane toads, imported into Australia early in the twentieth century, were reported in 2004 to be advancing in a vast deadly army on Darwin, posing a threat to household pets and children, for merely touching their toxic skins could prove fatal.

Large salt-water crocodiles still thrive in the Solomon Islands; when one 16ft monster was caught and killed in 2004, the remains of a local girl were found in its stomach.

When, in 2004, authorities in Bangkok sought to prosecute dealers illegally trading in exotic pets, the shopkeepers hastily disposed of their stocks of flesh-devouring piranhas not by killing them but by releasing them into the city's rivers and canals.

A rare delicacy among hillbillies in west Kentucky is a meal of grilled or stewed squirrel brains.

Upon seeing the ghostly figure of a gigantic bear emerge from the Martin Tower within the Tower of London in 1815, the sentry on duty lunged at it with his bayonet, then fainted. Found unconscious by his comrades, he was taken to hospital; when he was able to speak, he described what he had seen, but died two days later. During that time his bayonet remained embedded in the ancient timbers of the door.

Together with 6,069 scorpions, Malena Hassan occupied a glass box in a Malayan shopping centre for more than 32 days in 2004; only seven of her companions resented her presence by stinging her.

A headache can easily be cured, so the legend goes, by tying a buzzard's head around one's neck.

To ensure a firm hold of one's weapon in mediaeval sword fighting, sword-grips were bound with strips of fish-skin rather than ordinary leather.

Leopards haunted the outskirts of Bombay in 2004, attacking the unwary residents. A young man, sleeping outside in the cool of the

174

evening, was savagely mauled, while in another suburb of the city a four-year-old girl was dragged from the veranda of a house into the forest, where her half-eaten cadaver was found the next day.

Fishermen in the Indian Ocean take a model of a dugong (sea-cow) with them to ensure a good catch; it is filled with dugong grease and certain magical plants, and, when the maker dies, his leg-bones are secured to the charm, which guarantees even better fishing.

It is said that an elephant never forgets; nor do some horses, it seems, for in May 1821 a mare, with its rider asleep in the saddle, walked up to the stable door of Mr Salthouse of Scotforth, Lancashire, and was recognised as one stolen from him two years previously. Whether the rider was woken up and arrested, or the owner was so delighted at retrieving his property that he took no further action, is not known.

Getting the bird! As Dr John Milward was preaching in St Paul's Cathedral in April 1605, in the midst of his sermon a cuckoo came flying over the pulpit 'and very lewdly cried out at him with open mouth'.

In 2004 Austrian scientists discovered that octopuses, if not left- or right-'handed', at least have one tentacle that they tend to use more often than the others; they also have a favourite eye. Whether the scientists learned this by encouraging the octopuses to wink at them hundreds of times, or by repeatedly offering to shake 'hands' with them, is not known.

German police were alerted when a woman reported that her dog had been drugged, apparently by thieves who then stole euros to the value of more than £200; the investigation was called off when the animal started to regurgitate shreds of banknotes.

A chronicler recorded in January 1606 that 'in the City of London and surrounding shires, whole slaughters of sheep had been made, in some places the number of 100, in others less, where nothing is taken from the sheep but their tallow and some inward parts, the whole carcases and fleeces remaining behind. Of this there are sundry conjectures, but most agree that it tendeth towards those who make fireworks.'

The smallest fish in the world is the stout infantfish, found off the Great Barrier Reef, Australia; it would take one million of them to weigh a kilogram.

In 2003 a Bangladeshi woman was killed and swallowed up to her waist by a 10ft python as she collected fruit. The snake was killed and the body retrieved.

'Snakes and ladders' took on a new meaning in a town in Tyne and Wear in 2004 when firemen were called to a house to rescue a snake which had got itself stuck halfway through a wedding ring. A ring-tailed snake it wasn't!

In 1605 a merchant was punished for swindling by being sentenced to ride down certain streets on a horse, facing its tail, but one of the judges dissented from the others and suggested that the mount should be an ass, 'because that would cause more wonderment and attract a bigger crowd, and also the slow pace of the ass would prolong his punishment'.

In Washington a black bear proceeded to drink 36 cans of beer, then decided to sleep it off after climbing a tree. It was later lured down from its perch and trapped by using a bait it simply couldn't resist – more beer!

Vodka is a popular drink among Moscow residents but, because they give their pets more than an occasional sip, local vets often have to resuscitate drunken dogs, cats, and even budgies.

In the late 1800s some scientists believed that criminals were not actually killed by the electric chair but died during the subsequent postmortem. Professor William F. Z. Desant claimed to have invented a method by which electrocuted people and animals could be revived, and intended to verify it by applying it to 'a large, strong and healthy St Bernard dog, weighing about 150lbs.' Alas, the results were never published, if indeed the test ever went ahead.

CRIME CHRONICLES

The first time aircraft were used in the recapture of escaped prisoners was in 1932 when two convicts, John Gasken and Fred Amery, got away from Dartmoor Prison, only to be caught a week later.

No fewer than eleven police officers were murdered in Canada in 1962.

The last victim of the Spanish Inquisition was a Quaker schoolmaster, who was hanged in 1826.

The only woman in the USA to be executed for spying was Ethel Rosenberg, on 19 June 1953.

Whitney, a seventeenth-century entrepreneurial highwayman if ever there was one, offered to keep a major road into London clear of his brethren for £8,000 a year; it was not accepted.

Grave-robbers were also known as 'sack-em-up men', and in Warwickshire as 'Diggum Uppers'.

Edward Squire, a groom in the stable of Elizabeth I, attempted to kill her by smearing poison on the pommel of her saddle, and also on the chair used by her favourite, Robert Devereux. He failed, but the executioner, when using his disembowelling and quartering knife later, didn't.

One of the most notorious American serial killers to date is John Wayne Gacy, guilty of murdering 33 young men and boys, mostly by strangulation.

In the 1800s native workers who stole diamonds from South African mines by secreting them about their persons were beaten with sticks and had iron bands rivetted around their throats as evidence of their crime.

In the 1960s it was reported that the American FBI laboratories contained 2,500 shoe patterns, 1,750 US and foreign tyre patterns, 2,500 types of shoe prints and 42,000 different watermarks in paper.

When a hunchback attempted to assassinate Queen Victoria in 1842, scores of similarly deformed men were arrested and interrogated before the would-be killer was identified and imprisoned.

Two and a half million broadsheets were sold when James Bloomfield Rush was hanged for the murder of two men of the Jermy family in 1848.

Punishment by exposure in the pillory was abolished in 1837, the last victim was Peter James Bossy, who made an unwanted public appearance in one on 22 June 1832.

One of the biggest robberies in the UK took place in 2004, when over £26 million was stolen from a bank in Belfast.

At the Ascot races in the eighteenth century there were so many disturbances in the presence of royalty that a magistrate was ordered to attend and a room under the grandstand allocated as a courtroom.

Fingerprints are uniquely different, and so are pore prints, as was established by the Frenchman Dr Edmond Locard; sex is also identifiable, since female pore prints are smaller than those of males.

The first instance of hanging in chains occurred in March 1637, when one McGregor, guilty of theft, robbery and slaughter, was sentenced 'to be hanged in a chenzie on the gallows-tree till his corpse rotted'.

The earliest recorded hanging at Tyburn, London, was that of William FitzOsbert, known as 'William with the Red Beard', in 1196; he was guilty of sedition.

The last criminal in Aberdeen to be dissected after execution was Mrs Catherine Humphrey, hanged on 8 October 1830 for poisoning her husband.

Between 1535 and 1678, 160 English martyrs met their end in or near London. Of that total, 133 men were hanged, drawn and quartered, eleven were starved to death, five beheaded, four died in prison, one burned at the stake, one strangled, one died after torture and one was hanged. The total included three women, two of whom were hanged, the other beheaded.

The last occasion on which a person was whipped through the streets of Glasgow was on 8 May 1822, when a man was so punished for participating in a riot.

As many as fifty young women were believed to have been victims of Ted Bundy's murderous nature. When he was executed by the electric chair in 1989 a Tyburn-type crowd celebrated outside the penitentiary, some carrying placards proclaiming 'Burn, Bundy, Burn' and 'Thank God it's Fryday'.

The first occasion on which a traitor was hanged, drawn and quartered was in the thirteenth century when David, brother of Llewellyn of Wales, sided with the English against his native countrymen.

The last occasion in Europe on which a woman was burned alive was in Switzerland in 1782.

After 1757, victims of execution in France were no longer dismembered and quartered.

The last execution for high treason in Scotland occurred in 1820 when Andrew Hardie and John Baird were found guilty of conspiring against current voting regulations. The men were the last in Scotland to be sentenced to be hanged, drawn and quartered, although this was mitigated to being hanged until dead and then beheaded. The same method was adopted in England when the Cato Street conspirators met their end.

The first police officer to be killed while on duty was PC Grantham during an attempt to quell a street fight in Somers Town in June 1830.

Vienna no longer executed its criminals by breaking them on the wheel after the year 1786.

Sixteen enemy spies were executed during World War I: fifteen were tried in the Central Criminal Court at the Old Bailey, the sixteenth, a member of the German armed forces, by court martial.

The last woman to be hanged in public at Newgate Prison in London was poisoner Catherine Wilson in 1862.

Of the hundreds of rounds fired by police at the car containing the American murderers Bonnie and Clyde on 23 May 1934, no fewer than 167 of the bullets peppered the vehicle, killing the occupants instantly.

The last man to be hanged in California was Robert James, who was executed in 1935 for murdering his wife. After tying her down and trying without success to induce rattlesnakes and black widow spiders to bite her, he gave up and drowned her.

The *Chicago Herald* recorded that 9,800 murders, 132 judicial executions and 190 lynchings had taken place in the USA during 1894.

American FBI records contained 180 million sets of fingerprints in the 1960s, but the total increases daily.

It was not until 1830 that capital punishment for the crimes of horse stealing, sheep stealing, burglary and housebreaking was abolished in England.

The last execution in Canada took place on 11 December 1962 when Arthur Lucas and Ronald Turpin were hanged in Toronto's Don Gaol.

The first woman to be executed in Canada after its Confederation was Phoebe Campbell, hanged on 20 June 1872 for killing her husband with an axe.

The first person to be caught by the forensic DNA testing method was Colin Pitchfork, found guilty in 1987 of committing two murders, for which he received two life sentences.

Between 1788 and 1868 about 160,000 felons were transported from England to Australia as punishment for their crimes.

During the period 1805–1820 1,150 criminals were hanged, and their corpses used for the instruction of students in surgery. But as there were more than a thousand such students in London and about the same number in Edinburgh, and further schools in Liverpool and Dublin, the deficit was rectified by grave-robbers, human jackals who reaped fortunes by digging up the dead and selling them to the surgeons.

Canada executed 527 people between 1879 and 1945.

The last American pirate to be executed by hanging was Albert W. Hicks in July 1860. It took place on Bedloe's Island, near New York, and was witnessed by thousands of spectators. The celebrated circus owner P.T. Barnum saw the opportunity to obtain new exhibits for his side-shows; visiting the pirate in his cell, he gave him a new suit of clothes in exchange for the one he wore, and after the execution he arranged for a death mask to be made of Hicks' face.

Finland abolished capital punishment in 1824, Russia in 1947, Switzerland in 1875, Portugal in 1867, Italy in 1888 and Norway in 1905.

The last public hanging in Canada took place on 11 February 1869 when Patrick James Whelan, a Fenian, was executed for shooting the cabinet minister Thomas D'Arcy.

The oldest man to be tried for murder in the UK was 100-year-old Bernard Higginbotham, who, in 2004, cut the throat of his 87-year-old wife, after 68 years of marriage. It was deemed a mercy killing and he was freed.

The last man to be tried for piracy in Canada was James C. Douglas in 1865. He was mate on the ship *Zero*, the captain of which was brutally murdered, and although he received the death sentence, it was later reduced to life imprisonment.

Peter Heaman was the last pirate hanged in Scotland, the execution taking place in November 1821. Together with others of the crew, Heaman had murdered the captain of the ship *Jane of Gibraltar* in order to steal the 40,000 Spanish dollars carried as cargo; after the deadly deed the crew divided the loot among themselves, using a teapot as a measure.

The only judge ever to be sentenced to death in England was David Jenkins, who defied Parliament during the Commonwealth, when its members decreed that they, and not the king, acted with the authority of the law. Because he insisted that he as a judge owed his allegiance and acted (as now) with the authority of the Crown, not Parliament, he was charged with high treason and sentenced to death. He spent seven years imprisoned in the Tower, Newgate, Wallingford Castle and Windsor Castle, but regained his freedom on the restoration of the monarchy in 1660.

Hanged in January 1953, Marguérite Pitre was the last woman to be executed in Canada. She had been found guilty of delivering a package containing a bomb to Ancienne-Lorette airport. The bomb exploded in the aircraft, killing all 23 people on board.

Nearly a hundred felons were hanged every year in London and Middlesex in the 1780s, over 250 highwaymen being despatched at Tyburn between 1749 and 1771, not counting the many other petty thieves, pickpockets and burglars.

It was during the reign of George III (1760–1820) that branding was finally made illegal in England.

During the reign of King John (1199–1216) the owner of Baynards Castle, London, had the right to drown traitors in the Thames.

No fewer than 3,654,367 lashes with the whip were delivered to the naked backs of criminals serving gaol sentences in New South Wales and Van Diemen's Land between 1826 and 1840. Ouch!

The last man in Glasgow to be hanged in chains was Andrew Marshall, executed for murder in 1769. Before the birds could strip the flesh from the swaying cadaver, it was rescued by comrades and given a decent burial.

In legislation passed in 1779 by Gustave III of Sweden, capital punishment was abolished and replaced by the prisoner being flogged severely once a year, on the anniversary of his crime.

By an Admiralty Law of 1450 relating to the River Humber, any man who removed the anchor of a ship or cut the cable of a ship at anchor would be hanged at low-water mark. And any man who stole any ropes, nets, cords, etc., amounting to the value of 9d, would, at low-water mark, have his hands and feet bound, his throat cut, his tongue pulled out, and his body thrown into the sea.

Before the revolution of 1688, when William and Mary ascended the thrones, there were fifty offences that carried the death penalty; during George II's reign (1727–1760) this number increased to 113; by 1765 the number was 160, and by 1800 two hundred crimes were punishable by death. By 1939 there were only four, and today there are none.

Torture was not abolished in Scotland until 1708.

In the USA, from 1891 to 1897, there were 59,784 murders, 870 executions, 1,267 lynchings and 35,618 suicides.

During the reign of Edward I (1272–1307) 280 Jews were hanged for coining, while in the reign of Henry VII, 72,000 people were put to death for various offences. These were not the 'Good Old Days'.

The old custom of hanging in chains, whether alive or after being executed, was abolished by statute on 25 July 1834.

FOR THE RECORD

The first patent was taken out at the Patent Office on 2 March 1617 by Aaron Rapburne and Roger Burges 'who were graunted a privilege for the terme of XXI years of the sole makeing, carveing, describeing and graveing in copper, brass or other metalle, such and soe manie mappes, plottes or descripcions of Lond., Westm., Bristolle, Norwiche, Canterbury, Bath, Oxford and Cambridge, and the towne and castel of Windsor, and to sett forthe and selle the same.'

For the first time, a definitive book now exists, containing all relevant details of more than 8,000 prisoners held in the Tower between the years 1100 and 1939; compiled by Yeoman Warder (retd) Brian A Harrison and entitled *The Tower of London Prisoner Book*, it was published in 2004.

The first woman to die in Ohio's electric chair was Anna Hahn, in December 1938. Found guilty of killing George Gsellmann, she was suspected of poisoning at least twelve others.

The first man to use ether as an anaesthetic was Dr Long of Athens in Georgia, USA, in 1842.

To align the English calendar with that of Western Europe, eleven calendar days were omitted from the month of September 1752. This resulted in some rioting, people protesting that they had been robbed of eleven days of their lives.

187

The only triple execution to take place in Ayr, Scotland, occurred in 1817 when two men were found guilty of robbery and a third of fire-raising.

In 1839 a Sicilian youngster, Vito Mangiamele, demonstrated his prowess with numbers by calculating the cubic root of 3,796,416 in his head in 30 seconds.

The first railway in London was the London and Greenwich Railway, travelling over Southwark and Bermondsey on a viaduct of 878 brick arches.

The original name of the Blackfriars Bridge, opened in 1769, was Pitt Bridge, after William Pitt; Waterloo Bridge, opened in 1817, was initially called Strand Bridge.

The only king of England to be crowned twice was Richard I; it was decided that following his capture and imprisonment on the Continent, he should be re-crowned.

Mary was the first female sovereign of England, her coronation took place on 1 October 1553. Traditionally she should have been crowned by the Archbishop of Canterbury but, as he was imprisoned in the Tower of London for declaring Mary illegitimate, because of her father Henry VIII's annulment of his marriage to her mother Catherine of Aragon, Stephen Gardiner, Bishop of Winchester, deputised.

At the outbreak of World War II 62,244 Germans and 11,988 Austrians living in Britain were interned for reasons of national security.

In 1948 2.5 million cars were registered in this country and there were 4,513 road deaths. Now there are over 25 million cars and the annual total of road deaths is approximately five thousand.

The first time a condemned man was hanged, drawn and quartered at Tyburn was on 7 June 1594, the felon being Roderigo Lopez, a Portuguese, found guilty of attempting to poison Elizabeth I.

Flogging was not removed from the statute books of Delaware until 1972.

Louis XIV of France was born already equipped with two milk teeth.

Henry VI (1422–1461) was the only English monarch to be crowned king of France as well.

The largest opal in the world is the 'Halley's Comet'; found at Lunatic Hill, New South Wales, in 1985, it weighs 1,382.5 carat – 13.8 ounces.

The first reported use of Newgate as a prison was in 1211.

The first coffee-shops opened in London in the middle of the seventeenth century, and by 1710 there were more than two thousand of them. Only men were permitted to enter and partake, and it was not until seven years later that the Golden Lion admitted women, the first one to do so.

Indian Shridar Chillal allowed the finger-nails of his left hand to grow until they reached a length of more than 108 inches (starting from scratch!).

Scold's Bridles, or Branks, were first referred to in England in 1598, and last reported in Kendal, Cumbria, in 1834.

Queen Anne (1702–1714) was the only sovereign who had to be carried into Westminster Hall to be crowned, owing to her obesity.

Richard III, slain at the Battle of Bosworth on 22 August 1485 ('a horse, a horse, my kingdom for a horse!') was the only English king to be killed in battle.

The cadavers of hanged felons were first displayed as deterrents on gibbets in England during the reign of Henry III (1216–1272).

During the religious persecutions in France in 1546, during the reign of Francis I, about four thousand men, women and children were hunted from the glens of Languedoc and the Loire Valley and put to death.

The coronation of William and Mary in 1689 was the first time a king and queen were crowned as joint sovereigns in England.

In 1823 a Mr Ronalds took out a patent for an electric telegraph and proved its feasibility by passing messages through eight miles of wire, but when an offer was made to the Government to provide them with such a facility, they replied that 'Telegraphs of any kind are totally unnecessary and none other than the semaphores now in use will ever be adopted.'

Alice Stevenson, born in England in 1861, died in 1973, having lived for 112 years.

William Campbell is believed to have been the youngest person ever given a prison sentence in Scotland; on 6 November 1827, aged nine, he was imprisoned for eighteen months for theft.

During World War II the headquarters of MI5 was 58 St James' Street, London.

Reputedly the tallest man in the world, the American Robert Wadlow, who died in 1940, grew to 8ft 11in.

In 1669 two coaches took only two and a half days to travel between London and Leeds. This record was broken in 1776, when the same journey was accomplished in 39 hours.

The last fatal duel in England took place in Portsmouth on 20 May 1845, when Lieutenant Hawkey killed Lieutenant Seton.

The oldest chemist's shop in England is believed to be that in the market place in Knaresborough, which dates back at least to 1720.

Vietnamese Tran Van Hoy studiously avoided visiting the barber for thirty years, his hair eventually reached 6.2 metres in length.

For nearly six hundred years there was only one bridge crossing the Thames in London. Built in 1176, it was simply called 'The Bridge', and it was not until 1738 that another, Westminster Bridge, was built.

If you want milk in your tea but no milk jug happens to be available, send for Ilker Yilmaz, for in 2004 that Turkish gentleman set a new world record in 'eye-squirting'; sucking milk up his nose, he propelled it a distance of nine feet from his left eye, beating the previous record by three inches. Whether he missed the teacup or not is not known.

The last public execution to take place in Edinburgh was that of murderer George Bryce on 21 June 1864.

The longest beard in the world was that cultivated by a nineteenth-century Norwegian, Hans Langseth, reaching a length of 17ft 6in.

William Sharp, prevented from marrying his sweetheart Mary Smith by their respective fathers, retreated to a small room in the family house in Keighley, Yorkshire, and went to bed. There he remained for 49 years, eating well but speaking to no one, and hiding under the blankets if anyone entered the room. He died on 7 March 1856, his only words being 'Poor Bill Sharp!' Now that's what I call a sulk!

Edward VII was having so many problems adjusting his uniform before leaving the royal train at Rathenau on 9 February 1909 that the band present on the platform played the English National Anthem seventeen times in succession before he eventually appeared at the carriage door.

One of the earliest patents for improving weapons of war was a breech-loading revolving-barrelled cannon invented by James Puckle. It had different chambers for firing round bullets at Christian enemies and square bullets at Turks.

No fewer than 31 cows were struck and killed by a single bolt of lightning in Denmark in August 2004.

Scotland's last public execution occurred on 12 May 1868, when Robert Smith was hanged for the murder of a little girl. The noose had to be removed from his neck and readjusted, before the drop was operated.

The first person in Britain believed to have been struck by a falling meteorite was 76-year-old Mrs Pauline Aguss of

Lowestoft, Suffolk. Her husband found the astral missile, a small chunk of metallic rock, nearby.

The American Jones 'Siamese' twins, born in 1889, were unique at that time, in that their spinal cords were integral, rather than their heads or hips.

While the Marquis de Sade was incarcerated in France's Bastille prison, he wrote his book *The 120 Days of Sodom* not on single sheets of paper but on a single roll nearly 40ft long.

Dangerous sports are no new phenomenon. In May 1953 Major Christopher Draper, a 60-year-old ex-RFC pilot, not only flew a monoplane betwixt the upper and lower spans of Tower Bridge but continued upstream, flying under Waterloo Bridge, Westminster Bridge and twelve others. So impressed was the magistrate by the daring Major's exploit that he was discharged after paying £10.50 costs, rather than the possible penalty of £1,600 plus six months imprisonment.

The earliest recorded English lottery occurred in 1569, the top prize was £5,000, of which £3,000 was paid in cash, £700 in plate and the remainder in 'good tapestries meet for hangings [curtains, not executions!], and other covertures, and good sorts of linen cloth'. The tickets cost 10s each and were occasionally divided and sub-divided 'for the convenience of the poorer classes'.

Although the Roman Emperor Tiberius Claudius Nero (42 BC– AD 37) died of insanity after a dissolute and cruelly sensual life, in his younger days he was so strong that he could push his fore-finger through an apple.

When Eva Hofhauer got married in Korneuburg, Austria, in 2004, she wore what was probably the longest bridal veil in the world – it was 1.7 miles in length.

The first execution to be performed behind prison walls in Scotland was carried out on the murderer George Chalmers in Perth's County Gaol on 4 October 1870.

The heaviest human brain, recorded in 1975, weighed just over four and a half pounds.

AUTHOR'S DETAILS

Geoffrey Abbott joined the Royal Air Force as an aero-engine fitter prior to World War II. He saw active service in North and East Africa, Somalia and India, postwar in the Suez Canal Zone, the Hashemite Kingdom of Jordan, Cyprus, Malta, Iraq and the Gulf States, and later served with NATO in France, Germany and Holland. After 35 years' service with the RAF he retired in 1974 with the rank of Warrant Officer and then, on becoming a Yeoman Warder ('Beefeater'), lived in the Tower of London and was sworn in at St James' Palace as a Member of the Sovereign's Bodyguard of the Yeomen of the Guard Extraordinary, and by Justices of the Peace as a Special Constable of the Metropolitan Police.

As an author of many books on torture and execution, his qualifications are unquestionable. He once spent time in the condemned cell of the high-security Barlinnie Prison, Glasgow, and later stood on the 'drop' trapdoors in that gaol's execution chamber (as a fact-finding author, not a convicted criminal!). He also had the experience of having a noose placed round his neck by a hangman – the late Syd Dernley, a man endowed with a great, if macabre sense of humour!

Geoff, who now lives in the Lake District, has acted as consultant to international TV and film companies and has appeared in more than a dozen documentaries on UK and American television channels. By invitation, he has written the entries on torture and execution for the latest edition of the *Encyclopedia Britannica*. In addition to being Sword Bearer to the Mayor of Kendal, Cumbria, he is learning to become a helicopter pilot.

OTHER BOOKS BY THE AUTHOR

Ghosts of the Tower of London
Great Escapes from the Tower of London
Beefeaters of the Tower of London
Tortures of the Tower of London
The Tower of London As It Was
Mysteries of the Tower of London
A Beefeater's Grisly Guide to the Tower of London
Who's Who of British Beheadings
Lords of the Scaffold
Rack, Rope and Red-Hot Pincers
Execution
(also Japanese version)
Family of Death
Severed Heads
Crowning Disasters
Regalia, Robbers and Royal Corpses
The Executioner Always Chops Twice!
Lipstick on the Noose
William Calcraft, Executioner Extraordinaire!
A Macabre Miscellany